Self-Management for Adolescents

TREATMENT MANUALS FOR PRACTITIONERS
David H. Barlow, *Editor*

SELF-MANAGEMENT FOR ADOLESCENTS
A SKILLS-TRAINING PROGRAM
MANAGING EVERYDAY PROBLEMS
Thomas A. Brigham

PSYCHOLOGICAL TREATMENT OF PANIC
David H. Barlow and Jerome A. Cerny

Self-Management for Adolescents
A Skills-Training Program

THOMAS A. BRIGHAM
Washington State University

THE GUILFORD PRESS
New York   London

Library of Congress Cataloging-in-Publication Data

Brigham, Thomas A.
    Self-management for adolescents : a skills-training program / Thomas A. Brigham.
        p.   cm.—(Treatment manuals for practitioners)
    Includes index.
    ISBN 0-89862-202-6
    1. Self-management (Psychology) for teenagers.   2. Adolescent psychotherapy.   I. Title.   II. Series
RJ505.S44B75 1989
616.089'022—dc19   88-19031
                                                                          CIP

To my mother and father,
who helped me survive my own adolescence.

Preface

The following pages represent approximately 10 years of research, theorizing, and practice within the broad areas of adolescence and self-management. Although the issues are extraordinarily complex and often the stimuli for bitter debate, the objectives of the present book are relatively simple. The endeavor is to describe clearly and systematically a self-management program developed for working with adolescents so that other social scientists and practitioners can effectively replicate it in either research or treatment programs. Because of this focus, little effort is made to survey the extensive general literature on adolescents and the alternative approaches. Rather, the assumptions and rationale of a specific theoretical position, approach, and set of procedures are detailed. In candor, the effect might be labeled propaganda because it is designed to convince you both to recognize the soundness of the analysis and to try the program.

It is important to note that consistent with these goals, the book can be divided logically into two sections. The first section (Chapters 1, 2, and 3) reviews the basic assumptions about adolescence as a developmental period, presents an analysis of self-management, and develops a rationale for why self-management training is a logical approach for assisting adolescents who are having difficulties. The second section (Chapters 4 and 5) covers issues regarding teaching self-management skills in general and a specific set of instructional activities and procedures for the self-management program. The companion volume, *Managing Everyday Problems*, presents the actual instructional materials developed for teaching self-management skills and a general understanding of behavioral psychology.

The materials are "packaged" in this fashion so that you can easily acquire exactly what you need for your specific program. By separating the student materials from the theoretical analyses and instructor's guide, it is possible to make multiple copies of *Managing Everyday Problems* available at very low cost. Thus, whether you are counseling a small group of students or working with several classrooms, the needed student workbooks will be readily available.

The differences in the content and objectives of the instructor's manual and the students' workbook produce some problems for consistency of writing style. The first section of the instructor's manual, covering theoretical issues and problems of analysis, is written in a fairly standard academic style, but the second section and the students' workbook deviate from that standard. The section on teaching self-management skills is directed at you, the potential user, so I have chosen to use a more personal style. The task in the materials for the adolescents is to present a scientifically correct description of concepts and procedures in a form that is both enjoyable and useful. The form suggested in the American Psychological Association manual is not entirely appropriate, but it is hoped that these materials are literate and challenging without being dull or condescending.

In writing this book, I have come to recognize that while a large number of experiments have been completed, much research remains to be done. As a consequence, the reader is forewarned that many unanswered questions remain at the end of the presentation. I honestly do not view the program materials and procedures as finished products, nor do I view this incompleteness as a liability. As Barlow, Hayes, and Nelson (1984) noted in their fine book on the scientist practitioner, the systematic observations and insights of the practicing professional can make valuable contributions to program development and evaluation. For instance, I have already made several important changes in materials and procedures as a result of information from colleagues. This is then an invitation to join the ongoing research on how to help troubled adolescents by contributing the process and outcome data you might produce in using the program. For applied science, it is crucial to discover the problems, failures, and limitations of a particular procedure or set of procedures. Admittedly, news of failures will be emotionally less satisfying than news of success, but each will be equally welcome. In return, we will attempt to respond to your information and questions both personally and programmatically.

Although I am the sole author of the present book, many other people have made crucial contributions to the development of the program described in it. First and foremost Joan Jacobson-Brigham, my wife, has been an active supporter, collaborator, and invaluable critic throughout. Also our children, Jeremy and Christy, both teenagers, have provided many examples of what to do and what not to do when living with adolescents. In addition, they have read the materials numerous times and have made many good suggestions for their improvement. Another person very important to the development of the program was Professor Warren Garlington, who was a generous and kind colleague for many years. Other colleagues who have contributed to the development of the program are Don and Sherrill Bushell and Wesley Becker. Also, two very fine classroom teachers, Bonnie and Robert Hill, of the Clarkston, Washington School District contributed greatly. Without their exceptional abilities and commitment, the program would have failed in its first trials. Finally, a group of very talented graduate students worked with me over the years and did much of the actual research crucial to the program. There is no way of acknowledging adequately their contributions, but in order of appearance they were Joan Niemann, Alan Gross, Nancy Bologna, Jose Antonio Contreas, Christine Hopper, Armando de Armas, and Barbara Wood.

Many other people have assisted, and it is only possible to provide a generic thank you to them. Two further debts, however, must be acknowledged. Parts of this book were written while I was a Visiting Fellow at University College, Cardiff. The generous help and friendship of the faculty and staff there remain a model for me of collegiality, and they were greatly appreciated. Finally, the assistance and patience of Ms. Ruth Day in preparing the manuscript and the consistent support of both the Department of Psychology and the Washington State University in general are gratefully acknowledged.

Contents

Self-Management for Adolescents

1

Adolescents and Self-Management

Parent complaints and tall tales concerning toddlers, preschoolers, and elementary students are almost always countered with the warning, "If you think that's bad, wait until they get to be teenagers." Grandmothers and junior high school teachers seem to be especially good at terrifying parents with stories of adolescent atrocities. Then, of course, to many parents, these predictions appear to come true. Their normal if not exceptional child overnight turns into an ill-tempered, uncooperative, hostile, suspicious, unhappy, uncontrollable, unreliable, and unpredictable adolescent. The use of negative adjectives to describe the behavior of adolescents comes naturally to both parents and professionals. What is it about adolescence or adolescents that leads to this conception?

A Brief History of the Concept of Adolescence

The developmental period between late childhood and early adulthood that we now call adolescence is a relatively recent phenomenon. Historically, at puberty the individual passed from the status of child to that of adult, and most cultures had some form of ceremony or ritual to mark that passage. While it is beyond the scope of the present review to detail all of the reasons, in the industrial societies of Europe and North America, this pattern began changing in the 19th century. Increased productivity and general wealth reduced these societies' reliance on the labor of children and young people, which in turn led to the enactment of universal education acts and child labor laws. There is no doubt that such changes were positive for both the individual and the society as a whole.

1

Nonetheless, they initiated processes that have profoundly affected the status and treatment of youth, which continue to this day.

Although many circumstances of children and youth were changed by these processes, in all likelihood the most important was the increased period of dependence of the individual on the family and society. Even though the Latin root of *puberty* means adult, a person was no longer expected nor in many instances allowed to be independent at the onset of puberty. Increasingly, children were expected and required by statute to remain in school until older ages. The earliest universal education laws continued to at least implicitly recognize puberty as an important transition point by only requiring 6 years of compulsory schooling. By the beginning of World War I, however, 9 years of education was considered the standard in many areas, and in the period between the wars, many laws were enacted requiring individuals to stay in school until they were 16. In addition, the public school system in the United States was expanded to provide 12 years of instruction. Thus in approximately 100 years, the common definition of adulthood was changed from beginning at the onset of puberty to waiting until graduation from high school.

Concurrent with changes in the public school system, other forces in these societies further changed the way adolescents were treated. For instance, before World War I, when my father graduated from the 9th grade, he found a job in a retail business and moved out on his own. This was not unusual behavior; it was the social norm. His parents, the culture as a whole, expected him and the majority of his peers to be independent. In contrast, the 15-year-old who now attempts to leave school after the 9th grade and live independently is considered a truant/runaway and is subject to legal sanctions. These changes in cultural practices and expectations about what adolescents can or should do have profoundly affected the family structure and the psychological circumstances of the youth of our society. Many of the conflicts among adolescents, their families, and society in general result from this extended period of psychological and social dependence.

Adolescent–Parent Conflict

There are many sources of potential conflict between parents and adolescents, but two consistently reported by families having difficulties involve (1) discipline and (2) expectations of how the adolescent should behave. Both the adolescent and the parents recognize that he/she is no longer a child, but they tend to disagree as to what this means. The disagreement seems to center around the implications of this change in status. As a general rule, parents believe that because he/she is no longer a child, the adolescent ought to be more responsible. On the other hand, adolescents feel that they should be given more independence. In principle, these different expectations need not lead to family conflict, but in actuality they often do.

The basis of the conflict is the often contradictory interpretations given the notions of independence and responsibility by parents and adolescents. For adults, acting responsibly often means the adolescent's behavior should match some implicit standard of good conduct. Contained in this definition are such things as being home on time, increased contributions to the general maintenance of the home (yard work, dish washing, laundry, etc.), regular completion of school work, good judgment in the selection of friends and extracurricular activities, and keeping a neat and clean bedroom. In contrast, the adolescent wants to know why he/she must be home at a certain time; specifically what is the matter with her/his friends, and whose room is it anyway? And why can't I keep it the way I want?

Whereas parents tend to think of adolescent behavior in terms of ideals that they assume their adolescent must share, young adolescents want to know why something should be done in this particular manner at this specific time. Further, adult opinion may no longer carry the weight of injunction that it did for the child. For instance, the 12-year-old who responded positively to the request to make his bed and pick up the room may now as an adolescent question the need or validity of that request, "Geez mom, it looks OK to me, why does it have to be neat?" The compliant child has been replaced by the questioning adolescent who no longer accepts an explanation simply because it is given by a parent or adult. Parents often find this new pattern of responding very difficult to deal with and frequently become angry or upset in such situations.

A related and equally important source of adolescent–adult conflict is the adolescent's tendency to postpone doing anything/everything. This, of course, from the parents' perspective is a variation on the responsibility theme. The parent observes that it is 8 o'clock and the kitchen still has not been cleaned after dinner; the teenager responsible for kitchen clean-up is called and asked (instructed, enjoined, told, etc.) to immediately clean it. Rather than repentantly complying with this reasonable and appropriate parental request, the response is more likely to be "What difference does it make what time it's done as long as it gets done and why do I have to do it anyway? Sally/George never have to do anything around here." An objective analysis of any situation where one person requests that a second person stop what he/she is currently doing and do something for the first that the second does not particularly want to do suggests that the second will resist having to perform the specified task. The resistance usually takes the form of procrastination. Although the adolescent's procrastination can be objectively understood, even the most understanding parent will occasionally become infuriated at an adolescent's failure to get something done on time.

A final source of conflict is the failure of adolescents to recognize that in certain situations, parents and other adults have no sense of humor. A trait or instinct theorist might state that adolescents are naturally or instinctively sarcastic. A more systematic behavioral analysis can be provided for this pattern of verbal behavior. In their interactions with peers, sarcastic, obnoxious, vulgar, and obscene remarks occur in fairly high frequencies. Therefore, it is likely that the adolescent's usual response to a peer's question or comment will be of a form that most parents and other adults would consider inappropriate. If, as it often happens, an adolescent responds quickly to a parent's question, the response probably will be in the form used in conversations with friends. Most adults are naturally offended by such behavior. In my experience, there are few things that will make an adult furious faster than situations where it appears that an adolescent is laughing at or making fun of him/her. The adolescent in turn is both surprised and angered by the adult's reaction.

The Fundamental Conflict

Some psychologists have suggested that these and similar conflicts between adolescents and parents are the result of failures or breakdowns in communications between the parties. And certainly communication difficulties can exacerbate adult–adolescent conflicts. Nonetheless, the basic difficulty between adolescents and adults is not a failure to communicate. At the core of these many disagreements is a fundamental and very real conflict of immediate self-interest between the parents and society as a whole on one hand and adolescents in general on the other. The adolescent as an individual and adolescents as a group are capable of a wide range of activities in which we, as a society, have decided they must not be allowed to engage. As a consequence, we have a large and significant subpopulation whose range of behavior is being constrained by the society as a whole. This inherent conflict is manifest in many small areas as well as such major concerns as sexual behavior and use of alcohol, tobacco, and other drugs.

Freud, in *Civilization and Its Discontents*, provides a psychoanalytic view of the tension between the individual and the necessary constraints of society. Although much of the interpretation he gives may now be considered silly, his statement of the problem is very clear.

> The liberty of the individual is no gift of civilization. It was the greatest before there was any civilization, though then, it is true, it had for the most part no value, since the individual was scarcely in a position to defend it. The development of civilization imposes restrictions on it, and justice demands that no one shall escape those restrictions. What makes itself felt in a human community as a desire for freedom may be their revolt against some existing injustice, and so may prove favourable to a further development of civilization; it may remain compatible with civilization. But it may also spring from the remains of their original personality, which is still untamed by civilization and may thus become the basis in them of hostility to civilization. The urge for freedom, therefore, is directed against particular forms and demands of civilization or against civilization altogether. It does not seem as though any influence could induce a man to change his nature into a termite's. No doubt he will always defend his claim to individual liberty against the will of the group. A good part of the struggles of mankind centre round the single task of finding an expedient accommodation—one, that is, that will bring happiness—between this claim of the individual and the cultural claims of the group; and one of the problems that touches the fate of humanity is whether such an accommodation can be reached by means of some particular form of civilization or whether this conflict is irreconcilable. (Freud, 1930/1962, pp. 42–43)

While Freud was discussing the overall conflict between the individual and society, the further evolution of Western culture has made adolescence the main arena for this battle.

In presenting this analysis of the conflict between adolescents and adults, I am not suggesting that society's efforts to constrain adolescent behavior is incorrect. Certainly given the nature of modern society, adolescence as a period of extended dependency is essential for the individual's long-term welfare. Nevertheless, we must recognize that a conflict of immediate self-interests exists in the situation if we are to design effective programs to assist adolescents in trouble.

Resolving Conflict—Coercion

How then should society at large and parents in particular deal with adolescents, especially those already having difficulty adjusting to their status as adolescents? *Not* by physical or psychological coercion. There are a variety of philosophical and scientific reasons for opposing the use of force, but in the final analysis the evidence is quite clear: Coercion simply does not work.

Why Coercion Does Not Work

Putting aside questions of ethics in the use of force with adolescents, there are two fundamental reasons why coercion is not effective. The first is related to the adolescent's ability to exert countercontrolling responses. In the much misunderstood book *Beyond Freedom and Dignity* (1971), Skinner provides a systematic analysis of how the use of force or punishment to suppress a response or set of responses will occasion countercontrolling efforts on the part of the punished individual.

Countercontrolling responses take two forms. First, if possible, the individual will attempt to counter force with force. Many parents and youth workers have found their efforts to punish an adolescent met with physical or verbal resistance. In countercontrol, the adolescent attempts to punish the punishment response of the adult. Much family and institutional violence occurs as a function of attempts at punishment and the resultant countercontrol responses.

The second form of countercontrol is for the adolescent to escape or avoid the person or program that is trying to control his/her behavior. In situations where it is not possible for the individual to counter punishment with equal physical or verbal violence, the natural response is for the individual to flee the punishing agent and to try to avoid that person in the future. Although there are many possible valid explanations for the behavior of the runaway or truant, one of those is that the behavior is a form of countercontrol by escape and avoidance.

Finally, if the adolescent's environment is sufficiently constrained so that neither form of countercontrol is possible for a time, it is likely that emotional conditioning will occur in conjunction with the use of punishment. Punishment is an aversive process. The delivery of a punishing stimulus or the removal of a positive reinforcer contingent on the occurrence of a response elicits emotional respondents as well as suppression of the target response. It then follows that by the process of respondent conditioning (associative learning) the agent of punishment will come to be a conditioned aversive stimulus for the punished individual. Thus, the use of punishment in a constrained environment has the important negative side effect of making at least some of the adults in the environment conditioned stimuli capable of eliciting such emotional respondents as fear and/or hate. If these associations generalize to other adults outside the environment, these conditioned emotional responses then interfere with the adolescent's ability to interact with adults when he/she leaves the treatment program.

As suggested in the preceding paragraph, for coercion (punishment) to have a suppressing effect on the adolescent's undesirable responses, the individual environment must be severely constrained; that is, the program must control the major if not all sources of reinforcement or punishment. In the case of adolescents, however, this condition rarely holds. The adolescent typically interacts with a larger and more heterogeneous group of peers and adults. In addition, peers often provide a more immediate source of reinforcement and punishment; and for that reason, peer reinforcement and punishment frequently are more effective in controlling the adolescent's behavior than parents, teachers, or therapists. As a consequence, persons other than program agents are available who may reinforce or punish a diversity of both appropriate and inappropriate responses.

Even in institutional programs, short of 24-hour surveillance and/or complete isolation, it is not possible to eliminate these extraprogrammatic sources of reinforcement and punishment. An additional complication in the effort to control the environment is that staff are often inconsistent in their consequation of behavior. If reinforcers and punishers are delivered in an inconsistent or variable fashion, then schedule effects are likely to further interfere with the desired control of the individual's environment and behavior. In short, programs based on coercion are neither desirable in terms of their likely effects nor feasible in terms of the control required for their implementation.

In a certain sense, the present analysis has simply stated the obvious: Coercive institutional programs have not worked; the evidence is overwhelming (e.g., Gordon, 1981; Wolfgang, Figlio, & Sellin, 1972). Nonetheless, individuals and governments continue to advocate such approaches. It is therefore important to understand why they have not worked. Coercion, force, and punishment produce countercontrolling responses and conditioned emotional respondents. Both of these processes severely interfere with the adolescent's ability to interact with adults. Further, while it is possible in principle to achieve total control of an individual's environment in order to force behavioral change, procedural requirements for such control make its achievement functionally impossible. As a consequence, it is possible to assert with both empirical and theoretical confidence that not only have they not worked in the past, but also coercive institutional programs can not be made effective in the future.

Alternative Approaches to Resolving Conflict

Most psychologists certainly have long recognized the limitations and failures of punishment- or coercion-based programs and have attempted to develop alternative approaches. Overall, these efforts can be divided into two general categories, with a number of variations subsumed under each. Probably the largest number of programs designed to help adolescents would be broadly classified as educational or instructional. Here, the basic strategy has been to provide the adolescent with information, primarily about the consequences of the behavior(s) in question, in order to reduce the probability that the person will engage in that response in the future.

The second major grouping of programs all have some focus on directly changing the adolescent's response repertoire. These are discussed later in this chapter. The specific strategy used depends on whether the problem responses are viewed as the behaviors to be directly changed or as a result of some skill deficit. In the former case, the effort would be focused on changing the consequences for the problem responses and providing positive reinforcers for more desirable alternative responses. In the second instance, adolescents are assumed to lack some basic skill(s), and that deficit in turn leads to the difficulties they are having. The program is then designed to teach those specific responses to alleviate the problems. Because most programs involve some effort to intervene in the adolescent's environment to help correct specific undesirable responses, the differences between actual programs are often more theoretical than procedural.

Education to Change Attitude

Educational programs have been designed and implemented as efforts to deal with problems ranging from chronic delinquency to tobacco use. The educational strategy must by necessity implicitly or explicitly be based on the theoretical assumption that information and attitudes are the main determiners of behavior. Perhaps the most controversial effort to date designed to provide information and change adolescent attitudes has been the "Scared Straight" program initiated in New Jersey. This program received considerable national media attention because it intensively exposed delinquent adolescents to hard-core convicts (Lifers) who were imprisoned at the Rahway State Penitentiary. The language of the program was harsh, obscene, and brutal, and the objective clearly was to intimidate the adolescents. The participants' immediate reaction to the treatment was apparently the desired fear and revulsion. Unfortunately, this program and the variants which followed it have yet to demonstrate any long-term positive impact on participant recidivism rates.

Although considerably less extreme, alcohol information programs have also tended to emphasize the negative consequences of drinking behavior. A number of programs have been developed that begin the process of information and attitude formation in the elementary schools with the objective of preventing abusive drinking later in life. The majority of adolescents participating in alcohol education programs, however, are there because they have already had difficulty with alcohol. Such programs usually have a counseling element as well. In addition, if the participants have received a driving-while-intoxicated citation, aspects of punishment will also be involved. Nonetheless, information, information and punishment, information and counseling, and enforcement (punishment) programs have had little documented effect on drinking patterns, the age of onset of drinking, or drinking and driving behavior (e.g., see Hopkins, Mauss, Kearney, & Weisheit, 1987; Mauss, Hopkins, Weisheit, & Kearney, 1987; Meier, Brigham, & Handel, 1984). This is not to say that such programs do not result in increased participant knowledge about alcohol, alcohol effects, and changed attitudes toward drinking. Rather, these results indicate that it is appropriate to reject the hypothesis that information and attitudes are the major determinants of behavior.

This point becomes quite clear when the extensive literature on adolescent antismoking educational programs is reviewed. In many ways, smoking is the prototypical adolescent behavior problem. While cigarette smoking among adults has declined in the United States, the number of teenagers beginning to smoke has increased, primarily due to a dramatic increase in smoking among female teenagers (National Institutes of Health, 1976). In addition, the average age of the initiation of smoking is decreasing (Evans, 1976). This increase among youngsters has occurred in spite of a concerted effort by researchers to warn children of the dangers of smoking. The underlying premise of these early programs was that if children were informed of the adverse effects of cigarette smoking, they would choose not to smoke. While the goal of imparting knowledge has been achieved and children now are well aware of the health hazards of smoking (Evans, Rozelle, Mittelmark, Hansen, Bane, & Havis, 1978), this approach has failed to deter the onset of smoking.

The ineffectiveness of many teenage smoking prevention attempts may have been a function of researchers trying to apply adult-oriented programs to adolescents. When attempting to develop an effective smoking prevention program with youth, several important developmental factors must be considered. For example, emphasizing long-term health consequences of smoking may be effective with adults, but this approach fails with teenagers who are far more present oriented. Indeed, there is some evidence that emphasizing imminent physiological effects of smoking (e.g., increased carbon monoxide levels) and aesthetic changes (e.g., yellow teeth and/or bad breath) can be counterproductive, resulting in adolescent skepticism (Hansen & Evans, 1982).

The modal age at which daily smoking begins is now 12 to 13 years (Johnston, Bachman, & O'Malley, 1977). As noted earlier, the environmental importance of the peer group greatly increases at this age. The ability of peers to exert strong influences and pressure to conform is well known (Lewin, 1953; Sherif & Sherif, 1964). Rather than taking the risk of being excluded from one's peer group, a youngster under pressure may accept the offer of a cigarette in order to gain greater acceptance (Bland, Bewly, & Day, 1980). Indeed, peer pressure has been cited by students as the most potent factor influencing their decision to smoke (Newman, 1971). This observation has also been supported by systematic research (Biglan *et al.*, 1983).

Knowledge of the importance of peers in influencing youngsters to smoke has prompted some researchers to develop programs aimed at training children to cope with such pressures. Richard Evans (1976) and his colleagues at the University of Houston were the forerunners in developing and testing strategies based on countering social influences. Their "inoculation treatment" has produced mixed results (e.g., Evans *et al.*, 1978), possibly because of their reliance on adolescents viewing films depicting youths refusing cigarette offers rather than having the youngsters actually practice the pressure-resisting tactics. Researchers at Stanford and Harvard have found that role-playing enhances the learning of these skills (Perry, Killen, Slinkard, & McAlister, 1980). Furthermore, students who were trained to resist social pressures toward tobacco were less likely to begin smoking than those who did not receive special training (McAlister, Perry, Killen, Slinkard, & Maccoby, 1980). Even with this procedural improvement, however, success in preventing smoking initiation has been limited.

One problem with many of these "inoculation programs" is their narrow focus. Many of the pressures a child receives to smoke come not from peers, but from siblings and also via indirect (e.g., through modeling) or possibly by direct influences from parents who smoke (Biglan *et al.*, 1983). Training a youth to say "no" to an offer from a peer may not provide the at-risk individual with the skills necessary to handle these potentially more difficult pressures. Thus, the generalizability of these pressure-resisting skills is questionable. In addition, these approaches seem likely to succeed with those youth who do not want to begin smoking, but they would be less effective with those who desire to experiment or to take on the qualities associated with smokers (Leventhal & Cleary, 1980). Indeed, intentions to smoke among adolescents have been found to be related to the kinds of positive attributes that they associate with smokers (e.g., interest in the opposite sex, toughness, and precocity [McKennell & Bynner, 1969]).

Perhaps more importantly, smoking among adolescents is not an isolated phenomenon. Instead, early smoking is frequently associated with several other social and behavioral problems. Youth who begin smoking are more likely to have low grades and be truant from school (Bachman, Johnston, & O'Malley, 1981). Smokers have also reported less interest in school, less interest in learning, and more academic stress (Ahlgren, Normen, Hochhauser, & Garvin, 1982). Psychological factors such as low self-esteem, lack of self-confidence, and an external locus of control (McKennell & Bynner, 1969; Newman, 1971) have also been associated with adolescent smoking behaviors. These latter characteristics have been found to be related to an individual's general susceptibility to social inlfuences (Bandura, 1969; Rotter, 1972).

Thus, even such an apparently distinct problem behavior as smoking is the result of multiple factors in the adolescent's life and environment. Further, it is unlikely that it or any other adolescent behavior problem will yield to narrowly focused educational or technique-oriented approaches.

Education to Change Response Repertoire

As noted earlier, the second group of programs generally takes a more direct approach to dealing with adolescent problems. Rather than focusing on information or attitude change, these programs are designed to teach specific behaviors or to reduce the frequencies of others. For instance, the group home setting where a professional staff works with resident adolescents has been the basis of efforts to solve a wide variety of problems.

BEHAVIOR CHANGE

The group home approach is exemplified by Achievement Place, a community-based, family-style, behavior modification treatment program (Fixsen, Phillips, & Wolf, 1978). The treatment program utilizes a behavior deficiency model where behavior problems are seen as being due to a lack of appropriate skills. At Achievement Place, an attempt is made to establish behavior competencies for social, academic, and self-care skills. It is expected that learning these skills will result in the youth being more successful in his community. These new behaviors will result in obtaining reinforcers that were previously obtained largely through deviant behaviors (Fixsen *et al.*, 1978).

At Achievement Place, six to eight 12- to 15-year-old boys live under the supervision of the teaching parents. The teaching parents are a married couple who have received a minimum of 1 year of specialized training. They are responsible for the treatment, care, and management of the boys sent to Achievement Place by the Juvenile Court (Hoefler & Bornstein, 1975).

The youths living at Achievement Place attend the local school and frequently visit their natural homes on weekends and holidays. The activity schedule of the youths living at Achievement Place is not unlike that of other boys. It differs, however, in that Achievement Place is a token economy. The youths earn points for appropriate behaviors and lose points for inappropriate behaviors; these points are exchangeable for privileges. Using the token incentive system, the youths are taught social, self-care, academic, and prevocational skills (Fixsen *et al.*, 1978). The youths are eventually transferred from the point system to the merit system to futher enhance generalization effects. On the merit system, they receive all privileges free and are given social reinforcers for appropriate behavior. If appropriate behavior is maintained, the youths become eligible for homeward bound and are gradually transferred from the Achievement Place home to their natural homes. Using the point system, the Achievement Place staff has modified the boys' use of aggressive statements, tardiness, room cleaning, academic performance, and knowledge of current events (Phillips, 1968). They have also improved the boys' homework skills (Kirigin, Phillips, Timbers, Fixsen, & Wolf, 1977), conversational skills with adults (Maloney, Harper, Braukmann, Fixsen, Phillips, & Wolf, 1976; Werner, Minkin, Minkin, Fixsen, Phillips, & Wolf, 1975), negotiation skills with their parents (Kifer, Lewis, Green, & Phillips, 1974), employment interview skills (Braukmann, Fixsen, Phillips, & Wolf, 1975), and ability to accept negative feedback (Timbers, Timbers, Fixsen, Phillips, & Wolf, 1973).

In their evaluation of the Achievement Place treatment program, Fixsen *et al.* (1978) compared 18 boys who completed the Achievement Place program with 19 youths who had been judged as acceptable candidates for Achievement Place but instead were institutionalized. The posttreatment institutionalization rate for the Achievement Place youths was 17%. The reinstitution rate for the institutional treatment group was

37%. At the 2-year follow-up, these figures had changed to 22% and 47%, respectively. Twice as many youths from the institutional treatment group were receiving further institutional treatment after having completed their original treatment program (Fixsen *et al.*, 1978).

Recently, however, two extensive follow-up studies of posttreatment offense rates found that there were no significant differences between youths who participated in Teaching Family programs and those who participated in other programs (Jones, Weinrott, & Howard, 1981; Kirigin, Braukmann, Atwater, & Wolf, 1982). These results are of great concern because the Teaching Family approach to date has been the most carefully researched and documented of all the community-based behavioral programs. Because their approach has been so systematic, the results showing general positive effects during treatment have been replicated numerous times by other investigators employing variations on this approach (e.g., Liberman, Ferris, Salgado, & Salgado, 1975). Thus, although the Teaching Family Model clearly can be considered a success on many dimensions, some difficulties remain in terms of achieving their long-term goals.

A variation on the contingency management approach has been to teach the techniques to parents. Patterson (1974) gave parents a month of training during which they were asked to read the behavior modification training manual *Living with Children* (Patterson & Gullion, 1971). Along with the reading assignment, they were required to monitor the occurrence of a series of targeted deviant or prosocial behaviors. The parents also participated in training groups in which they observed models and role-played situations that illustrated the appropriate use of the procedures. Parents then carried out behavior modification projects designed to alter their youth's deviant behaviors. Patterson reported that the procedures resulted in a significant reduction in the youth's deviant responses. Similar findings using these procedures have been reported by Patterson and Reid (1973) and Wiltz and Patterson (1974).

Ferber, Keeley, and Shemberg (1974) used a treatment program modeled after Patterson's and reported less-impressive results. The authors stated that the youths demonstrated an improvement at the 2-month follow-up, but after 1 year, six of the seven families reported having serious problems with their children. Further, these investigators also suggested a number of problems associated with this approach: Families can constrain their interactions when the observer is in the home and, as a result, the observer will not be able to obtain an accurate sample of the target behavior; and it may at times be difficult to get parents to carry out the behavior modification procedures. A similar problem was encountered by Salzinger, Feldman, and Portnoy (1970), who suggested that a number of their treatment failures were due to the failure of the parents to carry out the procedures. Alexander and Parsons (1973) have also reported that parents often do not read the training manual. The reports on the use of contingency management with predelinquent and delinquent youths suggest that it can be an effective technique when the procedures are systematically applied. One of the difficulties associated with this method, however, is getting parents consistently to carry out the procedures.

SKILL DEVELOPMENT

Negotiations and Contracting. In the early 1970s, a third community-based behavior modification approach to the treatment of juvenile problems began receiving attention: teaching negotiation and contracting skills to families with delinquent children. Stuart (1971) suggested that much delinquent behavior is a result of dysfunctional family interaction patterns. These families are characterized by a general lack of reciprocally reinforcing interactions between parent and youth. In these families, such interactions mainly revolve around maladaptive behaviors (Alexander, 1974). Contracting and negotiation skills provide an alternative and, it is hoped, positive manner for family members to influence each others' behavior on a reciprocal basis (Alexander & Parsons, 1973; Kifer, Lewis, Green, & Phillips, 1974). A number of studies have reported positive findings using these procedures (e.g., Alexander & Parsons, 1973; Douds, Engelsterd, & Collingwood, 1977; Kifer *et al.*, 1974).

While these studies suggest that contracting is an effective treatment program for juvenile offenders, a number of investigators have failed to replicate the positive findings. Stuart, Jayaratyne, and Tripodi (1976) used contracting in an attempt to modify deviant behaviors of 60 youths. A therapist met with the youth and either his/her parents or his/her teacher and developed a behavioral contract. The 13 measures of effectiveness included school attendance, classroom performance, home behavior, court contacts, and satisfaction with the program. At the posttest assessment, only 4 of the 13 measures showed a significant improvement. The authors concluded that contracting alone may not be an effective treatment program for delinquents. Less than impressive findings have also been reported by Weathers and Liberman (1975) and Stuart and Lott (1972).

Social Skills. The most recent approach to dealing with delinquency is social skills training. Again, a form of deficit model is used to justify the approach. It has been observed that delinquent adolescents display clear deficits in interpersonal social skills (e.g., Freedman, Rosenthal, Donahoe, Schlundt, & McFall, 1978) and that children displaying poor social skills later have a very high frequency of adjustment problems, including delinquent behaviors (e.g., Roff, 1961; Roff, Sells, & Golden, 1972). These observations have led investigators to use a variety of procedures that can be broadly labeled social skills training with juvenile delinquents and other troubled adolescents (see de Armas & Kelly, 1987). Although the results of this work and that of others are promising, as yet no systematic posttreatment studies have been done regarding the impact of such training on the rate of juvenile offenses. Further, the majority of studies suffer from methodological problems that make it difficult to predict whether this will be an effective long-term approach (Spence, 1982).

In summary, while a number of fine programs have been developed within the context of both approaches, the overall results have been disappointing as measured by maintenance and transfer of trained skills to new settings and long-term outcomes (Feldman, 1983). One possible interpretation of these findings is that an important aspect of making long-term changes in behavior has not been dealt with in these programs.

Why Alternative Approaches Have Failed

Why has there been so little evidence generated showing clear unequivocal long-term effects? It is difficult to argue from nonexclusionary negative evidence. Nonetheless, it appears that the general conceptual model of adolescent problems is incomplete. To date, behavioral and social learning approaches to the analysis and modification of adolescent problem behavior have used some form of a skill- or response-deficit model. The adolescent is assumed to get into trouble in school because she/he lacks academic skills, has difficulties getting along with peers because of the lack of interpersonal or social skills, and loses control in the face of criticism because the person has no alternative ways of responding in such situations. Such a conception leads to programs that teach specific skills or responses to alleviate those deficits. Unfortunately, despite the face validity of this logic, teaching specific responses does not appear to be an effective way of producing response generalization or transfer of training (Stokes & Baer, 1977).

In their review, Stokes and Baer (1977) suggest seven methods for increasing the likelihood of trained responses generalizing to new settings. They are all ways of increasing the probability that the new response will be emitted and reinforced. A careful analysis suggests that these are implicit methods for teaching the individual to discriminate when the new response is both appropriate and likely to be reinforced if emitted. Along these lines, Catania (1976) interpreted the research on self-reinforcement in terms of discrimination. Simply put, he argued that the self-reinforcement per se is largely peripheral and that the important component is learning to discriminate when a response is good enough (appropriate) that it will eventually be reinforced by others.

The Self-Management Alternative

In the model of self-management behavior to be proposed in Chapter 2, the notion of response availability (behavioral competence) is combined with that of discriminative or analytical skills. Self-management requires not only the ability to emit a particular response or set of responses but also the ability to discriminate and analyze behavior–environment inter-actions to determine which set of responses is appropriate for the particular situation. Such discrimination skills increase the probability of rein-forcement of some of the self-management responses, thus making the whole class of responses more likely to be maintained and used.

This analysis suggests that the problem of transfer and maintenance of specific responses taught within the context of most programs might be dealt with by systematically teaching the discriminations (concepts) related to those responses. The relations between discrimination and concepts is exemplified by the work of Becker and associates (Becker, 1986; Becker & Engelmann, 1978). They have developed a powerful technology (Direct Instruction) that uses selected sequences of general case discrimination examples to produce generalized concepts and opera-tions that can be applied to many situations. Thus, there is a technology available for teaching concepts about responses as well as the responses themselves.

Given that a program should involve instruction in concepts about responses as well as the skills themselves, why should that instruction be in self-management as presented here? A major advantage of the self-management model is that it focuses on the individual and gives the adolescent a basis for understanding his/her own behavior. Adolescence is a period when the individual is attempting to learn how to deal with new demands. Instruction in self-management is therefore timely because it is an integrated system of concepts and procedures that enables the individual to generate solutions to novel problems. Finally, although the self-management model is based on a sophisticated theoretical analysis of human behavior, it translates to specific concrete concepts and procedures that the adolescent can master and effectively use.

The main objective of the self-management program developed at Washington State University is to provide the instruction, practice, and support that will enable students to change their own behavior. The program shows adolescents how to generate their own projects to deal with behaviors and situations they identify as being problematic. If we are effective in teaching those concepts and procedures, then it is likely that the adolescents will be successful in their own efforts. It then intuitively follows that if the adolescents generate their own successful self-change plans rather than having procedures or techniques imposed upon them by adults, they will be more likely to use such skills in the future.

The preceding analysis has focused on developmental and scientific aspects of self-management instruction, but a remaining reason for teaching self-management is simply that students enjoy it. In this program, adolescents have an opportunity to study and experiment on themselves. All of the program materials are written for, about, and with the assistance of adolescents. In our research, the large majority of adolescents report the program to be interesting, enjoyable, and useful. These positive evaluations mean that the students do not have to be coerced to participate in the program. In short, self-management training provides the adolescent with useful, effective problem-solving skills within a positive context in which the student is an active enthusiastic participant.

Addendum: On the Notion of Prevention

When adolescent problems are discussed, the strategy of primary prevention is frequently put forward as an alternative to treatment programs per se. Arguments are made for intervening with at-risk individuals or even all adolescents before major difficulties develop. Such an approach is justified by analogy to the successes in medicine in dealing with specific diseases primarily by inoculation. For instance, both smallpox and poliomyelitis have been all but eliminated world-wide via aggressive inoculation programs. By metaphorical extension, it is proposed that similar preventive exposure to information and experiences might be effective in reducing the frequency of many adolescent behavior problems.

At present, this general model of prevention is being tested by extensive research efforts in both alcohol and smoking education programs. Further, there is now an almost hysterical demand from government agencies and the public at large for drug education/prevention programs to help deal with the drug use epidemic. Although the various programs differ in regard to the specifics that students are taught, they share a common strategy of early and repeated instruction on the negative consequences of abusing these and other drugs, along with some form of training on "resisting temptation" and self-concept/image enhancement. Whether these programs will succeed in preventing smoking, drug, and alcohol abuse is, in the final analysis, an empirical question. But as noted earlier, the present results have been uniformly disappointing—indeed, so disappointing that Mauss *et al.* (1987) suggest that school-based prevention programs cannot succeed because they target relatively trivial variables (i.e., unimportant causally) in relation to other factors in the students' lives. Based on this finding, they propose that a community-based prevention strategy might be made to work. This is not an unreasonable proposal worthy of experimental testing, but an extensive review of the mental health prevention literature suggests that even this conclusion may be too positive. I now believe there are a number of fundamental logical and procedural errors in the general prevention approach that mitigate against its ever succeeding in any form.

In candor, this is a new position for me because the original impetus for the research program with adolescents came from working on adult self-control problems. It became clear that it was extremely difficult to get adults to change their behavior in any systematic fashion, and that it might be more effective to work with adolescents in an effort to prevent the development of such self-control problems in the first place. I still find the notion of prevention to be an extremely appealing concept, but upon careful examination, the basic analogy to inoculation is not very good.

All of the prevention programs reviewed to date, however, have either implicitly or explicitly assumed that the treatment, instruction, information, experience, and so on, they provide will inoculate the individual against acquiring the targeted response at some future time. As a medical procedure, inoculation is based on the body's immune system reacting to the introduction of a weakened dose of a specific disease organism by producing antibodies for that disorder. Later, the immune system then has a specific response that enables it to destroy the full-strength disease organism, thus preventing the development of the disorder. The development of an effective vaccine requires both the identification of an entity or condition responsible for the disease and a specific and lasting immune system reaction to that cause. While both of these criteria have been met in the case of many diseases (yellow fever and diphtheria are two more examples), there are other disorders where the inoculation approach has been less successful. For instance, cholera vaccines are only about 50% effective because not everyone has a permanent reaction to them. Further, there are disorders such as the many forms of cancer, heart disease, and stroke where as yet neither criterion has been completely met, nor is it likely they will ever be met. Scientists simply have been unable to identify single causal factors or even elementary etiologies. Rather, it appears that there are many factors that contribute in interactive and conditional ways to the development of these disorders.

Thus, research indicates that for these complex disorders there are classes of events, responses, and stimuli that increase the probability of a particular disorder developing and other classes of events, responses, and stimuli that decrease the probability. This situation clearly no longer fits the prevention/inoculation model and requires a new approach to reducing the incidence of those disorders. Physicians increasingly promote health maintenance behaviors, reducing exposure to hazardous stimuli, and changing cultural practice. But primarily, they attempt to promote good habits. In short, for many physical disorders, medicine has moved from a specific physiological/biological inoculation model to a model based on behavioral psychology.

Ironically, the majority of educators and behavioral scientists have not recognized this shift and continue to pursue an inoculation model of prevention for complex multiply caused human behavioral problems. Just as a particular form of cancer does not have a specific cause, behaviors such as smoking, abusive drinking, drug use, delinquent acts, suicide, and the like are all multiply caused. It then follows that it will not be possible to prevent them!

Despite the "good" intentions of the Congress and the federal administration, the massive amounts of money about to be spent on drug education will neither prevent nor reduce drug abuse. Short of major changes in cultural practices and the economy, the best that can be hoped for is to reduce the probability of those classes of events, responses, and stimuli that contribute to the development of drug abuse. The way to accomplish this is not by drug education but by increasing the probability of incompatible behaviors. Incompatible responses are those that cannot be done at the same time. For instance, with most people, eating saltine crackers and whistling are incompatible. Staying in high school and graduating are incompatible with dropping out. But the focus should not be to prevent dropping out, rather programs should be designed to increase those behaviors that contribute to staying in school. Let us be clear here about the point of contention. The argument does not assert that prevention is impossible—only that the conception has limits that must be recognized.

In the narrow view, the use of a condom will prevent teenage pregnancy, but the use of condoms or other contraceptive procedures is determined not by any single educational experience or authoritative injunction. Rather, the decision to use a condom, like the decision to smoke, is the result of multiple factors. These factors must be analyzed and manipulated if the specific response is to be affected.

In the case of most complex human behaviors, we have large sets of interacting responses that influence the frequency and patterns of those behaviors. This conditional aspect of behavior must not be ignored. The current prevention model tends to focus on the single specific response to be prevented, and that leads to strategies that cannot succeed. In contrast, the goal of the self-management skills program is to help individuals become happy, healthy, and productive. If the program materials and procedures are good and the course is effectively designed and taught, then the students will learn skills to help them control their environments and lives. Perhaps they will then live successful lives—perhaps not; but at the very least they will have a better chance than before.

2

A Theoretical Analysis of Self-Management

Some Questions

In the preceding chapter, I argued that self-management training was a viable approach to dealing with adolescent adjustment problems. Before describing the specific features of the program, however, it is necessary to examine the theoretical arguments and practical considerations that lead to its development. Interestingly enough, the first question is "Does self-management training require an independent theoretical analysis at all (i.e., does it involve any new principles or procedures)?" Although the answer to this question may appear to be intuitively obvious, in actuality that is not the case. I often have to ask myself if the procedures and processes being examined under the rubric of self-management really represent basic and important phenomena. Is there really a set of skills that are different from any other form of behavioral or standard clinical skills? The answer at this point is a tentative yes.

In the individual's application of behavior analysis skills to solve personal problems, there appears to be a sufficient shift in focus that the process requires an independent theoretical and procedural treatment. This, however, does not mean that we should abandon the careful, systematic, objective approach that led to the development of effective behavioral analysis and therapy procedures in the first place. Since the early 1970s, considerable effort has been extended in psychology on the development of self-control theories and therapies. The majority of these efforts have focused on the role of the self to the detriment of the clarity of the analysis and the effectiveness of the procedures. The following pages present the outline of a radical behavioral theory of self-management that has guided our research and demonstrate the practical advantages associated with this approach.

A Behavioral Language

> We know already that there is a time when the female fly prefers protein, which cannot nourish her own body, to sugar, which is an adequate food for her but useless for her eggs. Here is an example of survival of the individual being subordinated to survival of the species. *In some quarters it would be hailed as maternal instinct, and by so naming it we would be no nearer an understanding of what it is.* (Dethier, 1962, p. 71, emphasis added)

It may seem odd to begin an analysis of self-management with a quote concerning the eating patterns of the common fly, but Dethier's point is a general one about language and explanation, which is germane to the analysis of human behavior as well. In the past, I have used the terms "self-control" and "self-management" interchangeably (e.g., Brigham, 1978), and presently no general consensus exists in the general area of research and treatment that dictates how each term should be used. From a radical behavioral perspective, however, there are good reasons for using "self-management" to describe a particular type of response repertoire displayed by an individual and for reserving the term "self-control" solely to denote certain types of response contingencies that cause difficulties for the individual.

A major reason for preferring the term "self-management" to describe the behavior of the individual has to do with word usage. Clearly, the manner in which words are used has important implications for the analysis of the phenomenon in question. As Dethier (1962) and others (e.g., Rapaport, 1953) have noted, labeling often tends to be confused with explanation—especially when the label appears in the noun form rather than the adjective form. In common usage, the term "self-control" is consistently employed as a noun, whereas "self-management" more frequently appears as an adjective. For example, the sentence "Sally has a great deal of self-control," seems complete and stands on its own. Further, the statement can be easily interpreted as an explanation of Sally's behavior. On the other hand, "Sally has a great deal of self-management," is an awkward sentence and needs another word to complete it. The sentence is better rewritten as, "Sally displays a great many self-management responses or self-management skills." The term "self-management" itself tends to force the focus of the analysis on what the individual does. In contrast, the term "self-control" implies existence of a special entity called the self. After hypothesizing the self, the question "What does the self control?" follows. Again by implication, the self controls the individual's behavior. This interpretation of the term logically leads investigators to pursue an internal search for the self and its parts.

A related difficulty is that by focusing on the self, well-documented behavioral processes become transformed from observable environmental events to inferred cognitive events. Similarly, behavioral principles change from accounts of these observable events to speculations about hypothesized internal processes of a less defined character. The following illustration of self-reinforcement appears in a well-known text on self-control, after a careful and well-done presentation of positive reinforcement:

> A professor we know reported that he developed the bad habit of bluntly telling others when he thought they were not acting very intelligently. "What do you think reinforces this behavior?" he was asked. "I guess it's the feeling that I have that I am smart. By showing others when they do something dumb, it shows them that I am smart. The trouble is, of course, that it makes them angry." We suggested that he could gain the same reinforcer (feeling intelligent) by intelligently choosing a positive statement instead of making some deprecating remark. (Watson & Tharp, 1972, pp. 102–104)

Although the professor of the anecdote may have taken an initial step in a behavioral analysis of his actions (i.e., the observation that this particular response makes other angry), the difficulty is that here, apparently without notice, the definition of a reinforcer has changed from the observation of an environmental event to the identification of a feeling about behavior. Similarly, the basis for identifying a reinforcer has changed from a functional demonstration of an increase in the frequency of a behavior to an introspective analysis.

Clearly this manner of defining and identifying reinforcers alters the basis of explanation from behavior–environment interactions to the functioning of the internal self. Self-reinforcement is controlled not by environmental events, but by self-determined standards of performance, and those standards are inside the organism mediating the influence of environmental variables on behavior (Bandura, 1977). Whether the standard is inside the self is unclear at this time; but the opportunity to develop a new set of ids, egos, and superegos certainly exists here. Also apparently inside are self-instructions and discriminations. And what are these things? Thoughts, cognitions, cognitive states, and/or cognitive structures are some of the major candidates for the status of explanatory concepts (Meichenbaum, 1977). As some hypothetical self rather than behavioral processes become the target of therapeutic interventions, the clarity of the behavioral analysis is lost. Such ambiguity, however, could be avoided if investigators attend to the responses in question.

Now this may appear to be a strange position to take in an analysis of self-management. What can the term *self* refer to if not that collection of internal events, thoughts, feelings, and the like with which we are all intimately acquainted? I believe the candid answer at this point is that we simply do not know how internal events affect behavior. As a consequence, the term is used herein solely as a prefix to indicate the focus of the analysis. If one person analyzes a second person's situation and either suggests or implements a change, then, depending on the nature of those changes, we have some form of standard psychotherapy. If, on the other hand, an individual analyzes her/his own situation and systematically makes a change, then we have an example of self-management.

What then of the internal processes? Despite the general impression, thoughts, concepts, rules, feelings, wishes, desires, and the like are not ignored in a radical behavioral analysis, rather their analysis is approached with caution. Instead of theoretically assigning particular roles to such internal events, we attempt to discover their functional properties in self-management by building the analysis on already well-documented principles and procedures and focusing on the individual's responses. From a radical behavioral perspective, the question is not "What is self-control?" but rather "What does the individual actually do to manage his/her behavior?" From a radical behavioral perspective, the theoretical issue for psychologists should not be "What is self-control?" but rather "What does the individual do to manage his/her behavior?"

Obviously there are a number of issues concerning self-management where a radical behavior approach and analysis diverges from current psychological theories. As a first step in the elaboration of a radical behavioral position on self-management, three areas where a radical behavioral position clearly differs from other approaches to self-management are examined in detail. They are (1) self-reinforcement, (2) reciprocity, and (3) the role of conscious private events.

Self-Reinforcement

As interest in self-management approaches to behavior problems evolved in the late 1960s and early 1970s, one of the first procedures to be applied in this new approach was, not unexpectedly, positive reinforcement. In many ways, this choice was not unreasonable. Positive reinforcement has proven to be an extremely powerful technique in behavior modification programs, and the extension of the procedure to instances where the individual provides positive reinforcement for his or her own behavior seemed to be the next logical step. The logic and rhetoric of self-reinforcement have proven to be very popular; and currently, self-reinforcement is a key if not the major theoretical and procedural component of most conceptualizations of self-management.

Nonetheless, at this time, the focus of self-management systems on self-reinforcement appears to be overly simplistic. There are both theoretical and practical reasons why this emphasis seems misplaced. First, the origins of the concept of self-reinforcement are at least in part based on a misinterpretation of Skinner's discussion of the possible role of positive reinforcement in self-control (Skinner, 1953). For instance, a fairly common attribution to Skinner is found in the following passage: "Skinner (1953) suggests that one of the ways in which individuals control their own behavior is by the administration of rewards to themselves without environmental restrictions and contingent upon certain behavior" (Rehm & Marston, 1968). The most straightforward interpretation of this passage is that Skinner advocates self-reinforcement as a method of changing behavior. Skinner's actual verbal behavior was somewhat less positive.

After describing a possible example of self-reinforcement, Skinner goes on to analyze the example:

> Something of this sort unquestionably happens, but is it operant reinforcement? It is certainly roughly parallel to the procedure in conditioning the behavior of another person. *But it must be remembered that the individual may at any moment drop the work in hand and obtain the reinforcement. We have to account for his not doing so.* It may be that such indulgent behavior has been punished—say, with disapproval—except when a piece of work has just been completed. The indulgent behavior will therefore generate strong adverse stimulation except at such a time. The individual finishes the work in order to indulge himself free of guilt.
>
> The ultimate question is whether the consequence has any strengthening effect upon the behavior which precedes it. Is the individual more likely to do a similar piece of work in the future? It would not be surprising if he were not, although we must agree that he has arranged a sequence of events in which certain behavior has been followed by a reinforcing event. (Skinner, 1953, p. 238, emphasis added)

It is difficult to interpret this passage from Skinner as a suggestion that self-reward or self-reinforcement is likely to be an effective procedure for modifying one's own behavior. Skinner has noted the procedural similarity between operant reinforcement and self-reinforcement, but he has also recognized that some other process is required to account for the self-reinforcement behavior itself.

One of those processes must logically be self-deprivation. For a consequence to be a positive reinforcer for a particular response, it has to be delivered contingent on the occurrence of that response and generally not available at other times. In the case of the procedure labeled *self-reinforcement*, this means that the individual needs to abstain voluntarily from that consequence at other times. The self-deprivation requirement appears to be both the logical and procedural Achilles' heel of self-reinforcement. First, we must theoretically account for why a person would engage in self-deprivation, but even more difficult is teaching self-deprivation. This difficulty was forcefully called to my attention by a client who after politely listening to my instructions not to engage in a particular reinforcing activity until she had completed a specific response simply observed, "Dr. Brigham, if I could do that, I wouldn't need your help in the first place!" Upon reflection, I had to conclude that she was correct. I had not been teaching either self-deprivation or self-reinforcement, but rather placing external constraints on my clients' abilities to act in other ways, and this clearly was not self-management.

This experience caused me to reexamine the evidence concerning the practical question raised by Skinner about self-reinforcement procedures: "Do they work?" Currently, there seems to be a general consensus in the field that they are effective behavior-change techniques. One review concluded that "self-reinforcement is clearly one of the most powerful self-control procedures—effective when used alone, incremental when added to other procedures, and equal to or better than external reinforcement" (O'Leary & Dubey, 1979). Other equally strong endorsements of self-reinforcement are to be found in the literature. However, the evidence mustered in support of this conclusion does not appear to warrant such a positive assessment. In all, 10 studies are cited to support the thesis. Of these, only 2 were conducted in applied settings (see Baer, 1979, on the importance of applied research for testing principles); neither of these met the Bandura and Mahoney (1974) criterion on self-reinforcement—that the reinforcer be freely and continuously available to the subject whether the response is emitted or not. Most of the other studies are only tangentially related to the conclusions.

For instance, a study by Kanfer, Karoly, and Newman (1975) is cited as demonstrating that the statement "I am a brave boy (girl); I can take care of myself in the dark" was a self-reinforcer that increased the time children spent in the dark. Kanfer *et al.*, however, referred to the "I am a brave boy (girl)" statement as a verbal controlling response. The statement was not voluntarily emitted by the subjects contingent on any behavior, but rather was elicited by the experimenters on cue in the treatment condition. In fact, Kanfer *et al.* report that the statement was never verbalized by the subjects in the subsequent test sessions. They speculate that the children may have covertly emitted the response, but they indicated there was no evidence to suggest that the students actually did so.

A careful reading of the study's procedures indicates that the statement was never used as a contingent stimulus and, as Kanfer *et al.* note, it more likely functioned as some form of antecedent instruction to set a high criterion for staying in the dark. Such antecedent statements have been consistently demonstrated to affect behaviors (e.g., Hartig & Kanfer, 1973; Karoly & Briggs, 1978), and in the current analysis would fit within the context of environmental restructuring or commitment response. Irrespective of the precise theoretical interpretation of the procedures, the statement clearly had antecedent and not reinforcement functions. It is likely that the statement was judged to be a reinforcer because of its content, and not because of how it actually functioned in the study.

This negative view of self-reinforcement per se was recently confirmed by Gross and Wojnilower (1985). They found that there was no evidence to support the claimed effectiveness of self-reinforcement procedures in the absence of external constraints imposed by the investigator or therapist. Thus to date, unequivocal empirical evidence to support the notion of self-reinforcement as an effective applied procedure is nonexistent and certainly does not justify the major role the concept has been given in many treatments of self-management.

Again, it is important to be clear on this point. The argument is not that the procedure of self-delivering reinforcers can not affect behavior under certain constraints, but rather that it will not be effective when those constraints are removed. Because those are exactly the conditions under which we wish our students to be able to respond, training students in self-reinforcement would have very little practical value in the program.

As a consequence of these findings and theoretical analyses, it was concluded that self-reinforcement was neither an important nor a viable self-management skill. Instead, we decided to focus our instructional efforts elsewhere. Specifically, in regard to contingencies of reinforcement, we have concentrated on teaching students how to understand, recognize and change environmental contingencies.

Reciprocity

The concept of reciprocity is central to our analysis of self-management, but it has also caused considerable confusion about the role of the individual in behavior change. Simply stated, reciprocity refers to the mutual effects of two variables on each other: A may be viewed as the cause of B, while from a different perspective, B, may be considered the cause of A.

In psychology, it has been have suggested that the analysis of behavior as a function of environmental events is arbitrary and that changes in the environment may be analyzed in terms of changes in the organism's behavior (Bandura, 1971; Mahoney, 1974).

Reciprocity, in and of itself, is not a concept antithetical to a radical behavioral position. Skinner's basic definition of the *operant* consists of the effects that a response has on the environment and how those changes in turn influence the frequency of that particular response. The fact that psychologists generally concern themselves with manipulating the environment to produce behavior change does not rule out the possibility of other relations holding. The environment of an older nonlanguage child is considerably different from that of a child possessing functional language. If the nonlanguage child acquires functional language, that acquisition alters his/her environment in that what was noise is now the discriminative stimulus or reinforcement for words. Although applied behavior analysis may be more interested in the environmental changes that produced the language acquisition, it may be equally important to examine the environmental changes produced by the new language responses. In the second case, it is appropriate to plot the environmental changes as a function of behavior change. By doing so, it might be discovered that some classes of language responses produce greater environmental change than others. Such a finding, in turn, could be important for designing language-acquisition programs.

On analysis, the concept of reciprocity or the desirability of sometimes analyzing environmental change as a function of behavior change is not in question; in fact, this perspective is central to the analysis of self-management presented here. In order to understand self-management, it is necessary to view the environment from the perspective of the individual. Rather, the question of concern here is how the concept is sometimes used. Mahoney (1974) correctly argues that the notion of reciprocity need not result in the "mental way stations" so eloquently opposed by Skinner. Unfortunately, though, the conception of reciprocity frequently centers not on the behavior–environment interactions, but rather on the role of the individual's conscious cognitions in these interactions. For instance, the extensive locus-of-control literature often employs reciprocity as an explanatory concept; but, here, the individual's actual abilities to affect the environment are not systematically analyzed; instead, the individual's perceptions are examined. The importance of personal belief is illustrated with the following example:

> A child's poor school performance, for example, may be partly affected by his personally inferred incompetence. By systematically altering that percep-

tion, academic performance may improve. The future direction taken by the belief–behavior cycle may then be a function of myriad influences—whether the child incorporates his new experiential feedback into a modified pattern of self-statements, whether success experiences are appropriately scheduled to induce and maintain a resistant and enduring "internal" belief pattern, and so on.

What are my objections to this statement? On its surface it appears to be a sophisticated description of the relations between a child's academic performance, cognitive constructs (beliefs), perceptual processes, and success experiences. This, of course, is the difficulty with such propositions; they only appear to specify functional relations among these variables. When one attempts to determine whether the child perceives event *A* as a success experience or not, it becomes clear that there is no method available for either objectively or subjectively determining the event's perceptual status at that time. Thus, statements of this form are usually based on post hoc and largely intuitive analyses rather than on systematic data collected at the time. For those reasons, they can not form the basis of practical programs to systematically help people understand and change their own behavior.

In the past, the behavior analysis of phenomena proceeded and succeeded at the level of responses and environmental events. As the center of concern changes from such easily identified events, the likelihood of producing functional relations decreases. Clearly, recent theoretical speculation has shifted the concern from individual skills to vaguely identified individual beliefs, and in turn, the possibility of developing useful relations among variables diminishes. These arguments may seem to be essentially esoteric and of little practical relevance, but that is not the case. If one assumes an individual's beliefs about a particular situation are the causes of behavior in that situation, then those beliefs should be the primary focus of the program. If, on the other hand, as I contend here, beliefs are held to be a component of relations between the individual's behavior and environment, then the focus of the instructional effort should be on more functional aspects of these relations.

The case of reciprocity provides an interesting illustration of the benefits to be gained from this approach. If the concept of reciprocity is precisely defined as *the effects of the individual's behavior on his/her environment*, when one then examines adolescent behavior, it becomes quite clear that many adolescents do not recognize or discriminate this relationship. This then becomes a very important concept (belief) to teach. When adolescents begin to systematically observe how other persons react to the adolescents' own behavior, they become much more effective. Thus, reciprocity is a fundamental component of both the theoretical analysis of self-management behaviors and the instructional program.

Conscious Private Events

The appropriate role of conscious events is another important area of concern for a radical behavioral analysis of human conduct. As Skinner has frequently argued, the individual's verbal report of private events may reveal to the community at large the external events of which the behavior in question is a function. Unfortunately, imprecise conditioning operations produce the verbal repertoire for describing private events. Many times, in the process of acquiring a verbal repertoire, the relation between private events and external events is lost. As a consequence, both the individual and the community frequently fail to understand communications about private events. Speaking colloquially, however, the individual's verbal behavior can be used as an indication of that individual's current understanding about how he or she interacts with the environment (i.e., why the person believes he/she acts as he/she does). But do those reported beliefs cause the individual to act in that specific manner? It certainly seems reasonable to assert that beliefs, ideas, feelings, and so on do indeed cause one to act in a particular manner. But these private events themselves must be accounted for: "To say that a man strikes another because he feels angry still leaves the feeling of anger unexplained" (Skinner, 1953).

Further, after the analysis of the antecedents of such behavior, one must once again ask, what role do they actually play? Rachlin (1977) has argued that conscious events do not cause behavior, but instead tell about behavior–environment interactions. Similarly, Jaynes (1977), in an extensive analysis of consciousness, suggested that consciousness is not the same as thinking, but rather metaphorically represents the individual's experience in a fashion similar to a road map. Although road maps contain much useful, often essential, information, the road map per se does not cause the driver to engage in any particular behavior; it simply provides information about the alternatives. Upon analysis, the metaphors used in many psychological treatments of private events similarly lend themselves to a "road-map" or informational function for consciousness rather than a causal one.

For instance, Meichenbaum (1977), in discussing the internal dialogue, argues that it allows individuals to monitor their thoughts, wishes, feelings, and actions. This monitoring in turn causes them to behave in a particular manner. But to monitor means to observe or record the condition(s) of a particular system at a particular time. One does not say that a gauge measuring the changes of pressure in a system causes those changes. On the other hand, an observer discriminating the reading on the gauge may move to adjust some components of the system, thus changing the pressure.

To elaborate, in the area of nuclear reactor safety, how a technician reads the dials in the control room affects his or her behavior and possibly our future. It is not, however, the dials that cause a particular behavior by the technician, but rather the technician's prior experience and training with regard to those specific dial readings. Further, those dials must accurately reflect the condition of the system. The resultant difficulties in the reactor breakdowns at Three Mile Island were not caused by the technician's attributions, but by the fact that the dials did not accurately reflect the environment. Analyzing the problem from this perspective, while the technicians must know how to react to various dial readings, the major therapy for nuclear safety would focus on making sure the dials accurately reflect the environment.

Similarly, it is likely that many reports of private events do not accurately reflect behavior–environment interactions, and again the therapy would consist of teaching the appropriate discriminations to the individual. Because such an operation would involve the individual's verbal behavior, it might be interpreted as cognitive. Neverthless, it must be remembered that the individual's verbal behavior is changing, not because of some independent internal event, but because of the changes in behavior–environment contingencies.

The literature on self-instruction seems particularly to emphasize the internal aspect of procedures modifying behavior–environment interactions. For instance, one study compared cognitive self-instructions with contingency awareness and found that the self-instructions produced greater change in the target behavior of aggressive delinquent adolescents (Snyder & White, 1979). Although conservative, the authors concluded that "this suggests that treatment focusing on both external contingencies for desired behaviors and internal control of behavior by the use of private speech may be a potent behavior change strategy for aggressive delinquent adolescents" (p. 234). I am not going to argue here that teaching an adolescent a new set of discriminations about behavior–environment relations and the verbal responses to describe them is not a good thing to do. It is, in fact, an essential part of the self-management training program. Again, however, the interpretation of such results as a function of internal causes has the potential for shifting the focus of our efforts from teaching about behavior–environment relations to attempting to directly influence internal events.

In this particular study, the cognitive self-instruction group was trained to identify specific problem situations by emitting a verbal response chain and then to behave in a manner consistent with the instructions. The authors provide the following example: Situation—a cottage counselor says, "time to get up." Verbalization—"Already, damn. It feels good to stay in bed, but if I get up I'll get the points I need for cigarettes. OK, just open my eyes, get up. Good, I made it." Subjects were also reinforced with tokens for appropriate behavior. In contrast, the contingency awareness group simply discussed the various contingencies in the token system. Thus, the cognitive self-instruction group learned to respond to immediate and specific stimuli within the problematic situations while the contingency awareness group lacked such rehearsed stimuli or responses.

In analyzing and interpreting procedures, it is crucial that the focus remain on what was actually done. In this study, the adolescents were taught to discriminate a set of contingencies in their environment and were further instructed on how to verbally describe those contingencies. The difference does not appear to be one of behavioral variables versus cognitive ones, but again, to use Jaynes's (1977) metaphor, one of the scale of the map. The self-instruction group had the equivalent of a city street map, whereas the discussion group was given a correct but less specific road map for the state. It is easier to get around London with a street map of London that with a map of England that includes only the major streets of London. The verbal nature of the training operations and the label, *self-instructions*, naturally leads to an interpretation of the causal variables as internal. From a radical behavioral perspective, to be valuable, private events must serve a naming function or be discriminative for behavior–environment interactions. In summary, verbal discriminative stimuli undoubtedly were involved in the observed changes in the adolescents' behavior. However, those factors developed as a function of the systematic effort to teach them about current behavior–environment relations and will continue to serve only so long as the relations hold. Our objective in the self-management training program is to teach adolescents how to generate such analyses for themselves.

Self-Control Problems

Rather than focusing an analysis of self-management on the private events of individuals, from a radical behavioral perspective it appears more logical to begin with an analysis of those situations that cause difficulties for individuals. It was suggested earlier that these situations be labeled *self-control problems*. The majority, if not all, of the situations in which the individual is said to have a self-control problem involve some difference between the immediate consequences of a response and its delayed consequences.

Smoking is a good example of a response that has immediate positive consequences for most smokers, but accumulated delayed consequences that are clearly negative. Smoking is further complicated by the fact that even when the delayed negative consequences occur, they are not easily discriminated by the individual. That is to say, not only are there no clear immediate aversive consequences, but the delayed consequences for each response (identified by medical research) are so small that they cannot be discriminated by the individual. Later, when consequences such as coughing, sore throat, and shortness of breath do appear, smoking has been additionally strengthened by other behavioral processes to the point where the response is still difficult to eliminate when the consequences change.

A process that contributes to self-control problems is antecedent stimulus control. In the case of smoking, the response is easy to emit concurrently or in conjunction with other responses in a wide variety of settings. As smoking occurs consistently in many situations, these stimuli set the occasion for subsequent smoking. For example, many people smoke while drinking coffee. Because the two responses occur together, engaging in one may become a cue for the other. Later, when the smoker attempts to quit, the coffee provides a powerful antecedent stimulus for smoking.

Another example of a self-control problem based on a difference between immediate and delayed consequences involves going to the dentist. This instance appears to consist of immediate aversive stimuli and larger delayed aversive consequences. Here, the individual may not go to the dentist because the response is followed by some pain or discomfort and is therefore punished. Such small immediate aversive consequences are apparently sufficient to reduce the likelihood of going to the dentist until the delayed consequences of not going are felt. The resulting painful stimulation then forces the person to visit the dentist to escape that pain. If the individual had simply gone to the dentist in the first place, the delayed aversive painful consequences could have been avoided. These two examples indicate that the difference between the immediate and delayed consequences is a major variable in self-control problems.

To reiterate, in a self-control problem, there is some immediate consequence that has a controlling effect on the response, while there are later consequences for the response or alternative incompatible responses that have opposite effects from the immediate consequences. The adolescent who baits and argues with his sister is emitting responses that may produce some immediate small reinforcers. For example, the sister may become (1) upset and cry, (2) angry and shout, or (3) embarrassed and leave. In sibling conflicts, such outcomes often function as positive reinforcers. It is likely, however, that there will also be delayed negative consequences such as parental punishments for making the sister cry or later retaliations by the sister. Even though the brother may swear he will never do that again (apparently demonstrating a desire to change this behavior), it is likely that he will engage in similar responses in the future. If such behavior occurs often, we would say that this person has a self-control problem in interacting with his sister. As was the case with smoking, this particular example involves immediate positive consequences and delayed aversive consequences. Most problems of overconsumption (i.e., eating, drinking, smoking) appear to fit this specific set of contingencies. Both component contingencies must be present to produce self-control problems. If it were not for heart disease, lung cancer, emphysema, and the like, few people would worry about smoking. Thus, smoking would no longer be a self-control problem.

There are three other basic variations of these contingencies: A response may have immediate aversive consequences, but failure to make the response may have even larger delayed aversive consequences, as in the dental example. A similar set of contingencies is in effect when an individual whose initial social interactions have been punished in the past is, as a consequence, less likely to make social advances. Here, the reduction of important behavior by small immediate aversive consequences may lead to the long-range loss of greater positive social interactions with an increased sphere of friends and acquaintances (i.e., if the individual had emitted the approach responses, those responses may have led to the development of new friends and enjoyable activities). Finally, a response may produce a small immediate positive consequence, but not emitting that response and instead emitting an alternative response may produce a larger delayed positive consequence. Behavior such as saving money in small amounts may eventually result in the purchase of a large reinforcer, while spending that same amount immediately might produce only small reinforcers.

Although behavioral psychologists have tried to avoid analyzing phenomena in terms of nonresponding, it appears that nonresponding is an important component in analyzing self-control problems. In every self-control situation, the problem is a particular response that is either occurring or not occurring. As a consequence, it is important to examine the contingencies for both the occurrence and the nonoccurrence of the target response. The four sets of immediate and delayed consequences for the target response are summarized in Table 2-1. The first two instances are situations where the self-control problem is the occurrence of the target response, whereas in the second two, it is the nonoccurrence of a particular response that constitutes the problem. The contingencies in the

TABLE 2-1. Responding (R_1) and Not-Responding (R_0) Alternatives in Self-Control, and Consequences for Each Alternative

Response	Example	Immediate consequence	Delayed consequence
*R_1	Smoking	Minor reinforcing event	Major aversive event
R_0	Not smoking	No reinforcing event	No aversive event
*R_1	Spending money	Minor reinforcing event	No reinforcing event
R_0	Not spending money (saving)	No reinforcing event	Major reinforcing event
R_1	Going to dentist	Minor aversive event	No aversive event
*R_0	Not going to dentist	No aversive event	Major aversive event
R_1	Making new friends	Minor aversive event	Major reinforcing event
*R_0	Not meeting new people	No aversive event	No reinforcing event

Note. The problem response is indicated by an asterisk (*).

table are identified in terms of both stimulus and operation; a response can affect either a reinforcing or an aversive stimulus.

An important feature of self-management is made explicit by these examples. The immediate contingencies involve small consequences, either positive or negative, while the delayed consequences are all major but potential. Cases are well documented of individuals who smoked two packs of cigarettes a day throughout their adult life and who died of old age at 95 without any major health problems related to smoking. Similarly, regular visits to the dentist will not guarantee the avoidance of serious dental problems.

A less obvious aspect of self-management follows from the nature of the consequences for the responses that need to be changed. The required direction of change is a function of the immediate consequences: when the immediate consequences are positive (e.g., smoking, or spending rather then saving), the target response needs to be decreased in frequency; when the immediate consequences are negative (e.g., going to the dentist, or fighting shyness), the target response needs to be increased. To accomplish these changes, the individual obviously must use different strategies.

1. When decreasing the frequency of a response, a twofold approach appears to be effective. First, alternative incompatible responses that will produce reinforcement need to be found, and the individual must avoid situations that in the past were discriminative for the target behavior.

2. In the case of increasing the frequency of a response, the environment must be analyzed and restructured to make both the occurrence and the reinforcement of the response more probable.

These strategies are examined in detail later in the section on teaching self-management. But it is important to emphasize that the intuitively obvious self-punishment and self-reinforcement approaches both have been rejected on the logical and empirical grounds presented earlier.

The Changing Environment

The analysis of the contingencies involved in self-control problems, not unexpectedly, suggests that the environment plays a major role in self-management. A logical examination of the functioning of the environment in regard to the solution of self-control problems does, however, indicate that the usual conception of the environment and the corollary assumptions about how to change behavior are in need of modification. To indicate how the conception of the environment needs to be changed, the common assumptions concerning the role of the environment must be reviewed. Presently, the authors of introductory psychology texts often begin the section on behaviorism and learning theory with the equation $B = f(E)$. The generally accepted translation of the equation is that *behavior* is a *function* of the *environment*. This, of course, is a difficult statement to argue with. It is also totally gratuitous, because it does not specify *how* behavior is controlled by the environment. Most writers then go on to give examples from laboratory research of how the responses of an organism in an experimental chamber may be changed by manipulating aspects of the organism's environment. These instances of behavioral principles are extremely powerful, and by the end of the exposition the author has built a case for what may be called the behavior-modification or controlling-environment model of behavior. Greatly oversimplified, the major assumption of this model is that to change an individual's behavior, you simply change that individual's environment. The student comes away with the impression that the environment is somehow a monolithic, immutable force that molds behavior irrespective of other factors.

The concept of the controlling environment is either explicitly or implicitly held by many psychologists both inside and outside of operant psychology. What is wrong with this concept of the environment and behavior? Simply put, it is incorrect in its view of the environment. The usual criticism at this point is to say that the real environment is infinitely more complex than the laboratory one. That may be true, but it is not the critical error. The error is in how the typical laboratory environment is designed to be a primarily static one in which the organism's responses have no direct effect on the basic contingencies that the experimenter has scheduled. This is by necessity: In order for an experimenter to evaluate the effects of a particular variable on behavior, an experimenter must carefully control that variable and others. But the natural environment is not impervious to the effects of the responding organism; it changes.

At this point, the reader may object that the animal's behavior *does* interact with the experimenter's. The experimenter designs the environment, monitors the animal's responses in that environment, and changes the environment when appropriate. These activities of the experimenter represent a major advance in the methodology of the experimental analysis of behavior. This interaction of the investigator with the experimental organism is an important feature of inductive research (Sidman, 1960; Skinner, 1956). Careful monitoring of the organism's responses allows the investigator to manipulate an independent variable and directly observe the effects on the animal's responding. Thus, the laboratory environment does change in a systematic manner related to the organism's responses. But there are two differences between changes in the laboratory environment and those in the natural environment. The first is simply the immediacy in both small and large ways. This, of course, is mainly a difference of degree, but the importance of immediacy of a consequence contingent on a response is well documented. Similarly, it is likely that the immediacy of change plays an important role in the functioning of the natural environment.

The second difference is also one of degree and has to do with a behavioral interpretation of the concept of reciprocity. It is clear that the relations between the organism and its environment are dynamic and reciprocal. The environment changes the organism's behavior, but it is changed by that behavior in turn. This is especially true for humans, where the important environment consists, for the most part, of other humans. In these situations, the organism–environment distinction changes with perspective: One individual's responses most likely are another individual's stimuli.

There is, of course, a similar reciprocal relation between the experimenter's behavior and that of the experimental organism. But there is a form of insulation between the experimenter's responses and the changes in the organism's behavior; changes in the organism's behavior are systematically transformed, quantified, and analyzed, and therefore may have an impact on the experimenter's behavior only in remote and indirect ways. Although these processes may carry the weight of scientific method, they can lead to the view that changes in the environment are separate from changes in the experimenter's behavior. The conclusion is that the environment has changed the organism's behavior, but it ignores the complementary change in the environment (the experimenter's behavior) produced by the changes in the organism's responses. The reader may recognize the preceding analysis as a statement of psychological reciprocity discussed earlier in the chapter.

Although this concept of the interaction between behavior and the environment is not a radical departure from current operant theory, the differences are important for the analysis of self-management. Skinner, in his analysis of operant behavior, has often focused on the effects of responses on the environment. One reason he selected the term "operant" was because the response *operates on* the environment. By implication, to operate means to affect, to produce results, to change. Therefore, this informal definition of the operant implied that the response changes the environment (Skinner, 1953). In his more formal discussion of the operant, however, Skinner chose to give a heavier weight to the role of the environment. Here, it is the environment that affects the response, that is, changes its frequency. Thus, the operant becomes a response whose future probability of occurrence is a function of its stimulus consequences. But again, in his discussions of countercontrol (Skinner, 1948, 1974) and self-control (Skinner, 1953), he takes the position that the individual can change his or her own environment. Finally, Skinner (1953) contends that ultimately, the environment determines behavior:

> If this is correct, little ultimate control remains with the individual. A man may spend a great deal of time designing his own life—he may choose the circumstances in which he is to live with great care, and he may manipulate his daily environment on an extensive scale. Such activity appears to exemplify a high order of self-determination. But it is also behavior, and we account for it in terms of other variables in the environment and history of the individual. It is these variables which provide the ultimate control. (p. 240)

What is to be made of these apparent inconsistencies in Skinner's position on the role of the environment? The problems are resolved by recognizing that these statements represent different levels of description in Skinner's analysis of behavior. As a consequence, it is possible to hold as a major theoretical assumption that it is the environment that ultimately controls behavior, but still to assert that in the day-to-day operation of the environment, the individual can change the environment by behaving.

Unfortunately, both critics and practitioners of the analysis of behavior too often focus on Skinner's statements about the environment as the ultimate source of control and ignore other aspects of his analysis of behavior. For the applied behavior researcher, especially those working with adolescents, however, Skinner's positions on countercontrol and on the ability of the individual to change the environment are as important as his assumptions concerning the ultimate role of the environment in controlling behavior. To elaborate, when someone is taught a new skill, two things happen: The individual's behavior is changed by an environmental manipulation, but it also becomes possible for the individual to change the environment. In self-management, augmenting an individual's ability to deal with the environment should be of more concern to the behavior analyst than changing behavior by manipulating the environment directly.

The behavior modification conception of the environment continues to be held widely because of its manipulative and explanatory power. When an experimenter places an organism in a particular environment arranged in a specific manner, it is an extremely powerful reinforcer for the experimenter if the organism's behavior conforms to a predicted outcome. Likewise, the application to human problems of those principles and procedures derived from the laboratory has been extremely successful in many instances. Numerous examples of such successes can be found in the *Journal of Applied Behavior Analysis, Behavior Therapy, Behaviour Research and Therapy,* and other journals. Also, there has been a very practical reason for the environmental emphasis in both laboratory and applied research: To date, it has been easier to manipulate the environment directly because more knowledge is available for isolating and manipulating environmental variables than for dealing with individual variables.

This position, however, appears to be reaching a point of diminishing returns as the sole basis for behavioral research and programs. An examination of many successful behavior modification research programs shows that they have involved powerful consequences in relatively constrained environments. For example, Lovaas's (1973) research with autistic children used powerful reinforcers and punishers in an extremely controlled environment. This in no way negates the achievements of Lovaas and his associates but simply puts that research into the context of the behavior modification model. Violating the constraints and assumptions of the model greatly reduces the applicability of behavior modification procedures if innovative corrections are not undertaken.

Reppucci and Saunders (1974) found just these sorts of difficulties in their research at the Connecticut School for Boys. Their initial conception of the project was to design an environment that they would control to "shape up" the boys' behavior. In designing their programs, they appear to have assumed that their work with the boys represented a closed system, in that no one would interfere with their control of the boys' environment. Unfortunately, the behavior of a variety of individuals—boys, administrators, politicians, and others—failed to match the investigators' expectations and impeded the operation of their controlled environment. Because they were unable to manipulate the environment as they had expected, they then concluded that the assumptions of the operant model about how to change behavior did not work and that what was needed was a new form of social psychology.

Such an out-of-hand rejection of an operant approach appears inappropriate because many programs, such as Achievement Place, have overcome these difficulties. In the Achievement Place program (Fixsen *et al.*, 1978) environmental changes are considered and adaptive self-management skills are taught. But as a consequence, this overall program and its procedures more closely fit the proposed model of the *changing* environment than that of the *controlling* one. Similarly, until the recent work on self-management procedures, the adult with minor to moderate adjustment problems who was still operating in the natural environment was generally outside the domain of behavior modification or behavior therapy. This was the case primarily because the assumptions about how to change behavior (i.e., making systematic changes in the environment) could not be made to operate in that individual's environment.

A further important but distinct issue, not adequately considered in most early behavior modification models, is the question of generalization. Clearly there is no guarantee that behavior changed as a function of controlling the environment in one situation will be maintained in subsequent situations. The problem of generalization of behavior modification programs such as token economies became an important theoretical and practical issue. In general, it was assumed that once the individual's behavior had been changed, the changed behavior would automatically occur when appropriate in new situations or environments. Again, this assumption did not prove to be correct. Readers interested in a more extensive treatment of this problem should consult reviews such as Stokes and Baer (1977) or Karoly and Steffen (1980). Also the problems of generalization or transfer of training are discussed here later in regard to the design of the self-management program.

In general, because the model used in much behavior modification research has not adequately considered the interaction between the client and the modifier, the method for dealing with problems in applied projects has been to attempt to gain more control of the environment. As indicated earlier, however, such attempts have been counterproductive. Because of its emphasis on the reciprocal interactions between organism and environment, an analysis of the environment as proposed here makes it possible to anticipate these difficulties and to develop noncoercive procedures for dealing with them. For example, when the teacher is no longer considered an impervious controlling environment for the children in a class, the teacher will be taught in advance how to respond appropriately to the countercontrolling responses of the students, the principal, and other teachers. The logic of a changing environment and the corollary emphasis on the individual's ability to change the environment is a major premise of a behavioral model of self-management.

Finally, the conception of the environment presented here frankly questions the degree to which someone can directly intervene in the environment to change behavior. This practical limitation can be illustrated by considering the difficulties presented the psychologist by a child with a behavior problem versus a predelinquent adolescent. In the case of the younger child, it can be (and has been) reasonably assumed that the child's parents and teachers control a significant portion of his/her environment. The strategy typically adopted in such a situation is to teach the parents and teachers how to modify the child's behavior. The success of such an approach is well documented. On the other hand, a number of investigators have ruefully found that such a strategy has little chance of success with the adolescent. The environment of the adolescent is not as circumscribed as that of the young child. No single adult or set of adults control all or a major portion of the adolescent's environment; a wide variety of consequences are available from a heterogeneous peer group. Also, the adolescent's ability to engage in countercontrol behaviors is much greater than that of the young child. As a consequence, the intervention strategy must change from a behavior modification focus on directly changing the environment in order to change behavior, to one of changing behavior to modify the broader patterns of behavior–environment interactions. This strategy may be called *indirect behavior modification* or, in this instance, self-management training.

For indirect behavior modification, or self-management training, the environment must be viewed as consisting of two parts: that of the therapeutic setting and that of the larger environment where the new behaviors must be maintained. In the therapeutic environment, the therapist has much less powerful techniques available to influence behavior (modeling, logical analysis, and social reinforcers), and therefore, somewhat paradoxically, he/she must teach clients more powerful techniques for modifying their own behavior: self-management skills.

A Model of Self-Management Behavior

The preceding sections have detailed the differences between a radical behavioral perspective on self-management and that of other approaches. It is now time to specifically outline the implications of these differences for a model of self-management. Self-management is the ability of the individual to systematically affect his/her interactions with the environment. Self-management, as conceptualized in this manner then, is the application of behavior analysis principles and procedures to modify the behavior–environment interactions *of* the individual *by* the individual. That is, rather than behavior modification being viewed from the perspective of the environment, the person whose behavior is being changed and the person doing the changing are one and the same. The target of the analysis and modification at any one time can be the individual's response repertoire, his/her environment, or frequently both. For clarity, these procedures can be classified in terms of their function in the self-management process as being either concerned with analysis or modification of the problem response.

The following model of self-management behavior involves some basic assumptions about the environment and motivation implicit in the previous discussion that need to be made explicit here. The abilities to analyze, modify, and evaluate behavior–environment interaction are not used unless there are sufficiently good reasons to do so. That is, motivational contingencies for self-management responses must be present in the environment. Negative reinforcement (escape or avoidance of some aversive condition) was suggested by Skinner (1953) as the major reason for engaging in self-management behavior. Thus, I might wish to control my eating behavior because I am embarrassed by my heavy appearance. Nonetheless, while strongly motivated to change my behavior, I may lack the skills to do so. Consequently, people frequently have self-control problems because they lack the required skills to deal with those problems. However, occasionally an individual will simply lack the motivation to engage in self-management responses. Irrespective of the theoretical interpretation of this lack of motivation, in those instances, the procedures proposed here will be ineffective. Further, if the new behaviors (products of self-management efforts) do not make contact with appropriate contingencies, they will not be maintained. Consequently, it is assumed in the following treatment of self-management that the proposed skills will all be developed and maintained as a function of the individual's interaction with his/her environment.

This may seem to be a trivial point, but it is a crucial one for the operation of the self-management program. The self-management program we have developed, and similar programs, are essentially instructional in nature. While it is possible to use contingency management procedures in the training program to help students learn self-management skills, their use will depend on environmental contingencies largely beyond the control of the instructor. This means that instruction in self-management will be ineffective if the individual's natural environment outside the program (family and peers) is unlikely to provide the positive reinforcers to maintain those new behaviors. This problem is discussed in greater detail in the section on teaching self-management.

Analysis

The most important component of a behavioral analysis approach to changing behavior is reinforcement. A central task of self-management, then, is to learn to analyze the environment in terms of reinforcement contingencies. Catania (1976) interpreted the research on self-reinforcement in terms of discrimination. Simply put, he argued that the self-reinforcement per se is largely peripheral and that the important component is learning to discriminate when a response is sufficiently good (appropriate) that it will eventually be reinforced by others. Returning to the example from Skinner, the student may indulge him/herself in some reinforcing activity after completing a task because he/she has learned to discriminate when that work will be reinforced by others. The interaction of the individual's behavior with the consequences in the larger environment maintains both the working behavior and the self-reinforcement behavior. From this perspective, the first component in self-management is the ability to discriminate (analyze) the various behavior–environment interactions in one's own life. Without this set of analytical responses, the individual cannot effectively use any of the other self-management skills.

The major behavior for analysis in self-management is self-observation. Self-observation can consist of the systematic recording of behavior and its antecedents and consequences to analyze the behavior/environment interdependencies, or simply noting another person's reaction to a particular response or set of responses as a way of determining how to interact with the person. The individual with many self-management responses is skillful at analyzing his or her own behavior and that of others. An important part of analyzing the other person's responses is the ability to understand what things reinforce the person's responses. The individual can then discriminate the various contingencies for both his or her own responses and those of others in the environment and can emit the appropriate responses.

Related to the ability to observe one's own behavior–environment interactions is the recognition of mutual influences of the individual's responses on the environment and the effect of the environment on his or her responses. This, of course, is again the concept of reciprocity. In the case of self-management, it refers, in the first person, to the recognition that how I behave affects the way people react to me, and vice versa. Although this may appear to be an overly simple point, people vary tremendously in the degree that they understand it. In general, individuals characterized as lacking self-management skills or having self-control problems display little or no understanding of this essential interdependency.

Finally, an important product of the ability to objectively observe one's own behavior is the understanding of personal private events. The individual skillful at self-observation can discriminate the relations between behavior–environment interactions and private feelings. The individual who can recognize the source of his or her feelings of anger in the behavior–environment interplay has a much greater chance of dealing with the problem than the individual who can only report feeling angry. For example, smokers often report one of the reasons they cannot stop is a periodic overpowering urge to have a cigarette. Such urges seem to be beyond their control and without any cause that they can understand except that they need a cigarette. However, when the person learns to identify the antecedents of the urges, he/she is then able to manipulate the environment to reduce their frequency. As a consequence, it is then much easier to stop smoking.

The person who possesses these analytical skills will then be able to recognize the various immediate and delayed contingencies involved in self-control problems discussed earlier. The student's recognition that he/she is not studying enough because other incompatible responses are immediately reinforced by some friends, while the consequences for studying are delayed, constitutes the first step in solving the self-control problem. Similarly, the adolescent who understands that some friends provide the immediate consequences for illegal drinking by encouraging and reinforcing those behaviors may then be able to take steps to change the problem behavior. The person characterized as having many self-management skills will be able to analyze the immediate and delayed contingencies in the environment and deal with self-control problems accordingly.

Modification

Obviously, the ability to analyze would do the individual little good without the complementary skills of being able to modify behavior–environment interactions. How does one modify the personal environment? Although a wide variety of procedures might occasionally be used, the core of modification skills consists of the reinforcement, extinction, and shaping of other people's behavior and restructuring of the physical–psychological environment. An example of environmental change by reinforcement and extinction is provided by special-education students who were taught to change their social and educational environments (Graubard, Rosenberg, & Miller, 1974). Special-education children often interact with a hostile environment that has labeled them deviant and, therefore, as people who can be treated with less respect, subjected to more ridicule, or given more negative comments. Graubard *et al.* taught a group of special-education children some simple reinforcement and extinction techniques. They showed them how to reinforce the positive comments of teachers and "normal" students. For example, the children were taught to make the "uh huh" ("I understand") response when a teacher carefully explained something to them, and to thank the teacher and praise the teacher's efforts. On the other hand, the students broke eye contact after the teacher's negative comments and were generally unresponsive to them.

Similar procedures were used with other students in the school. These procedures involved the systematic manipulation of the therapeutic environment, which in turn made the students more skillful in manipulating their environment. For instance, when the special-education children used their new social skills, there was an increase in positive comments and approaches and a complementary decrease in negative ones by the teachers and "normal" students toward the special-education children. The special-education students, by changing the way they used reinforcement and extinction, changed their environment and made further positive changes possible. In addition, their changed behavior changed the teacher's environment and that of other students, because the special-education children were now a source of social reinforcers.

It is appropriate to reiterate here that such an approach will only succeed if the new behaviors fit the environment. If, for some reason, there had been other powerful contingencies on the behavior of the teachers or other students to maintain their negative responses to the special-education students, then the procedure would not have worked. Graubard *et al.* (1974) appropriately labeled their approach an environmental or ecological one. Because the special-education students were not taught how to analyze their environment and behavior, the Graubard *et al.* study is not an example of self-management per se. Rather, it represents the successful implementation of one component of the self-management model. Individuals can, however, be taught these skills within the context of self-management training with similar positive results (e.g., Gross, Brigham, Hopper, & Bologna, 1980).

In summary, one set of procedures used to modify the environment, and thus the individual's own responses, consists of the techniques of behavior modification. An additional important set of self-management skills not usually considered within the context of behavior modification or behavior therapy involves restructuring the physical–psychological environment. Skinner's initial analysis of self-control focused heavily not on consequences per se, but on environmental structuring involving either the physical or psychological environment. It was assumed that the individual could arrange the environment so that the probability of particular responses would be increased or decreased. In line with the earlier analysis of the environment, he further assumed that if these changes were successful, there would be environmental consequences to maintain the new behaviors. Although this approach to self-management has not been systematically examined with humans, there is animal and anecdotal evidence to support the analysis.

For example, Kanfer and Phillips (1970) relate the story of Odysseus and the sirens as an instance of arranging the physical environment to prevent a particular response. Odysseus, of course, plugged his sailors' ears with wax and then had himself lashed to the mast so that he could hear the sirens' song without losing his life or his ship. A more recent anecdote involves a personal problem solved by a rearrangement of the environment. After many years of setting up reinforcement or punishment contingencies for the automobile riding behavior of our children with limited success, an analysis of the environmental situation suggested an alternative approach. Although the goal of strong familial affection that transcends situational variables is a desirable long-term objective, a realistic assessment of the probability of such behavior under the stimulus situation of a crowded back seat suggests it is extremely low. The obvious solution ("obvious" is a *post hoc* term; it took many years of trying contingencies before a restructuring approach was taken) was simply to change the adult–child seating patterns. Under the new arrangement, the driver and one child sat in the front while the second child and an adult sat in the back.

Many miles were covered in relative comfort and peace maintained by small reinforcers, in contrast to the small amount of control exerted by contingencies employed in the past. The difference was that the change in the environment eliminated the "accidental" kick or bump, the "friendly" poke, and so on, which had led to retaliation and escalated verbal and/or physical violence. These behaviors were the key to the self-management problem. When they occur, the probability of disruptive inappropriate responses is increased irrespective of whatever consequences may be programmed. A few years later, to check if the observed changed behavior was due to increased maturity on the part of the children, a *brief* reversal was instituted. While they did behave somewhat better than in years past, there was nonetheless an easily discriminated increase in disruptive behaviors.

Although the anecdote is presented to illustrate environmental restructuring per se, it is appropriate to examine it as a self-control problem. From the perspective of this chapter, these interactions were causing problems for both me and my children. Their inability to meet the requirements of my "reasonable" contingencies and ride without the various forms of fighting frequently lead to my making loud threats of bodily harm and occasionally carrying them out. Because I prefer to characterize my behavior as calm, logical, and reasoned, such responses on my part were personally aversive. Thus, the patterns of responding to the immediate situation by all of us represented personal self-control problems.

This quasi-experiment convinced the author that environment restructuring can often be more efficient and effective than the manipulation of consequences. Similarly, the impact of environmental changes on behavior can be seen in the simple instruction to smokers to keep all cigarettes and ashtrays put away before and after smoking. The manipulation changes the environment by removing stimulus factors that in the past had cued smoking, and it introduces a delay between the desire to smoke and the availability of a cigarette. These small steps consistently result in a 25% to 35% reduction in the smoking frequency below baseline (e.g., Danaher & Lichtenstein, 1978). Certainly, additional changes are required before the individual can stop smoking, and the environmental restructuring must be maintained by appropriate contingencies. Nonetheless, small environmental changes can play an important role in the solution of self-control problems.

Rachlin's research on the commitment response with animals provides more solid experimental evidence for this approach. The focus of analysis is on commitment responses. These responses commit the organism to engaging in a response that is incompatible with the problem response. In the standard situation, the consequences for these two potential responses result in the organism emitting the problem response. But in the commitment response approach, at an earlier time, the organism has an opportunity to emit the commitment response before the onset of the situation in which the problem response typically occurs. The commitment response is followed by a different set of stimuli in the presence of which only the alternative (desired) response can occur. The key to this interpretation is that preferences vary over time. The alcoholic, while sober, is more likely to make a commitment to abstain from drinking if the next opportunity to drink is sometime in the future than if the opportunity is immediately at hand. Thus, if the environment can be arranged appropriately, the organism will emit the commitment response and the desired response in turn. Rachlin and Green (1972) demonstrated these relations in an experiment in which pigeons, when given the choice of responding for immediate 2-second access or delayed 4-second access, preferred the immediate consequence. From an analysis of the combined gradients of delay and magnitude, it was predicted that if the pigeons were forced to make the choice 10 seconds in advance of the opportunity to earn an immediate or delayed reward, they would choose the larger but delayed reward. In general this prediction was confirmed. Rachlin and Green suggest that *when invented by an individual*, the commitment response paradigm may be a viable self-management technique.

Finally, the psychological ecology literature provides a rich body of research bearing directly on how to affect behavior by structuring the environment, research that is largely ignored by behaviorists. Although the position and research are too extensive to cover here, the essence can be summarized as follows: More-accurate prediction of behavior in a particular situation can be made from knowledge of the behavior setting (physical–psychological structure) than is possible from knowledge of the individual characteristics of the person entering that setting. Specifically, as Barker (1968) has argued,

> While it is possible to smoke at a Worship Service, to dance during a Court Session, and to recite a Latin lesson in a Machine Shop, such matchings of behavior and behavior settings almost never occur in Midwest (Oskaloosa), although they would not be infrequent if these kinds of behavior were distributed among behavior settings by chance. (p. 46)

In short, the physical–psychological environment plays a major role in determining behavior, and behavior change can be facilitated by environmental restructuring.

Returning to the self-control problem of the adolescent who was frequently fighting with his sister, how might that individual modify the environment to deal with the problem? The first step would be to analyze the problem situation: Do they fight all of the time, or is there a particular situation where they tend to fight more often? Suppose, for instance, he observes and discovers that he is more likely to start baiting and provoking his sister when she starts boasting about her grades. Having identified a stimulus control variable, what might he do next? He should explore alternative ways of acting–responding in that situation. What would happen if instead of baiting, he were to praise her for the good grades? Would she respond positively in return? We do not know, but it might be worth a try. Another possibility would be simply to leave the situation for a number of times just to change the pattern of interaction (break up the stimulus–response chains). Whatever he does after several interactions, he should evaluate how his new behavior is affecting her. As a more positive relationship develops, then further changes could be made in his behavior. It is important for the adolescent to be able to analyze the situation and his behavior and understand that by changing his own behavior he can affect the interaction. These proposed steps do not represent a piecemeal approach; rather, each step can be derived from the principles outlined in the analysis of self-management skills and self-control problems. Although different problems and environmental situations require different sets of responses to change the behavioral–environmental contingencies, those responses also follow from a similar process.

At this point, it is important to emphasize the systematic theoretical nature of this analysis. Self-management as conceptualized here is not a collection of techniques to be used in a piecemeal fashion. Instead, the person who has learned self-management can analyze problems, select and implement appropriate interventions, and evaluate the results.

At the risk of confusing the distinction made earlier concerning a radical behavioral approach versus other approaches, our self-management program may be described as concept or rule based. Skinner (1966) has discussed the aforementioned activities as examples of rule-governed behavior and provided a framework for their analysis. More recently, Becker and associates (Becker, 1986; Becker & Engelmann, 1978) have presented an extensive behavioral analysis of how to design and teach what they called "concepts about objects–events" and "concepts about operations." Our instructional strategy is based directly on this analysis.

In summary, self-management consists of objectively analyzing your own behavior, discriminating contingencies of reinforcement and punishment, understanding the notion of reciprocity, and restructuring or changing the current environment. I recognize that at points in this chapter, the issues of concern may have seemed tangential to the goal of helping adolescents, and, further, my positions are often quite different from standard psychological thought. Irrespective of the idiosyncratic nature of the treatment, the issues are important and demand your careful consideration. What I have attempted to establish is a systematic theoretical position from which the program assumptions and procedures can be understood. There is an old rural saying, "The proof of the pudding is in the eating." In other words, something may have looked good, but we were always more interested in how it would taste. Specific to the topic at hand, a self-management theory may sound good, but does it generate a program that works? I endeavor to answer that and to further document the advantages of this approach in the next chapter.

3

Evolution of the Self-Management Program

The self-management materials and procedures prescribed in the next two chapters evolved over a period of approximately 10 years of research. Our initial effort was quite modest and occurred as a secondary experiment in a larger research program supported by the National Institute of Mental Health. The objective of the main program was to examine how students' academic performance would be affected by being given more control over their classroom environment (Brigham, 1979). The results clearly demonstrated an important and significant improvement in academic achievement, but there were no observable effects on the students' general self-management skills. This latter finding was very disappointing, so Dr. Joan Niemann and I decided to see if those skills could be taught directly.

Basic Design Decisions

Operant Learning Theoretical Model

At the very beginning of this experiment, we made a number of decisions that influenced the long-range development of the research program. First and foremost, the theoretical model selected to guide the research was operant learning theory. This decision reflected both personal and empirical factors. The personal reasons admittedly played the major role because my training and past research had been within the context of the experimental and applied analysis of behavior. At that time, however, the movement in psychology toward cognitive-based theories was gaining strength, and the cognitive learning theories certainly represented an alternative theoretical base. Nonetheless, on careful examination, much of the rationale for these approaches was based on the a priori assumption that a behavioral model could not account for cognitive phenomena, but there seemed to be no actual evidence to support this assertion. At approximately the same time, Bandura (1977) was forced to recognize that while the explanations of behavior change were becoming more cognitive, evidence was accumulating that performance-based (behavioral) methods were more effective in actually producing behavior changes. Thus, current cognitive theories were actually very poor at differentially accounting for behavioral phenomena. Bandura went on to propose a theory based on the notion of self-efficacy, but one could, with equal legitimacy, interpret this observation as indicating the weakness of cognitive theories and pursue the analysis of cognitive processes from a radical behavioral perspective (e.g., see Skinner, 1966). For whatever reason, the adoption of behavior analysis as the theoretical model has been a clear benefit to the program. To this point, applied behavior analysis has proven to be a systematic and effective base for the research in self-management and has provided a logically consistent technology for analyzing and changing behavior that adolescents can understand and use.

Concept Based

The second decision, to a certain degree, followed from the first, in that the program was designed to be concept or rule based. At first glance, such an emphasis might seem to be the antithesis of a behavioral approach, but it is quite consistent with the analysis of the role of discriminative stimuli in complex human behavior as presented in Chapter 2. It also follows from this analysis that the many instances required to teach a concept may contribute to the generality of that stimulus class. Because at that time there was accumulating evidence that technique-oriented programs were not producing good results in terms of generalization and/or maintenance of treatment effects, focusing both on rules and on the specific target responses appeared to be a viable alternative approach.

Natural Science Context

Finally, it was decided to use the introductory laboratory science course as a model for the instructional approach to be used in the program.

There were a number of reasons for the selection of this pedagogical model, but fundamentally, it focuses the instructional effort on the responses the student must make to translate the concepts and processes into experimental procedures. It forces the instructor and curriculum designer to ask what the student must be able to do to complete this experiment or unit. Similarly, it shifts the emphasis from (1) the instructor lecturing to (2) the student discussing and doing. In general, research has demonstrated that this is the most effective teaching strategy. Further, examining human behavior and adolescent problems within a natural science context facilitates the development of a more objective and less egocentric perspective. As a final added bonus, the simple experiment makes an excellent model for generalized problem solving.

Rationale

The preceding rationale for these decisions was, of course, developed after the fact. If forced to justify these assumptions at the time, the reasons would have been similar but less formal, and they probably would have been presented in a more defensive fashion. Now, after 10 years of research, no systematic evidence has been produced that would lead to the rejection of these major assumptions. This is not to say that none of the procedures, materials, or strategies have been changed as a function of research results; that clearly has occurred. But overall, the results have been consistent with the initial assumptions. This does not, however, prove that this theory is correct and alternative ones wrong. Rather, to this point, there has been no reason to reject them, and so they continue to be tentatively held.

An Early Experiment on Generalization of Self-Management Skills

As noted at the initiation of the first experiment, these views, while less developed, affected the design of that study. In designing the study, the following questions were considered: "What should be taught?" "How should it be taught?" "How should program effects be measured?" In the first instance, very little information was available about self-management/self-control at that time, so it was decided to start with basic operant principles and procedures and then try to demonstrate how they might be used to deal with one's own behavior. Over a 10-week period, 13 topics were covered, ranging from measurement and definition of behavior, reinforcement, and discrimination to self-management of obesity and planning a self-management project. Because no written materials were available, the course was taught in a modified lecture–discussion format in which study guides were handed out to the students at the beginning of the class session. The study guides helped the students identify the important information and facilitated student participation. The next class session consisted of some sort of laboratory demonstration of the procedures just discussed. Finding appropriate dependent measures for the study presented an interesting logical problem. The standard sorts of knowledge of operant principles and self-management were used, along with student-designed self-management projects, but how can one demonstrate that the student uses the skills outside the training setting?

The question of whether students use the ideas and procedures outside the specific program assignments and influences is actually the key measure of whether the individual has acquired any self-management skills. The completion of a self-management project under the implicit or explicit direction of the instructor is a good training exercise, but it in no way guarantees that the students use those skills in other situations. We decided to set up a situation where the self-management skills would be useful but also where there was no obvious connection to the self-management program. This was accomplished by establishing a classroom management system called the "Good Behavior Game" (Barrish, Saunders, & Wolf, 1969) in a math class in which these students were also enrolled. This game is a method for consequating groups for the individual member's behavior. The class is divided into two teams, and individual instances of inappropriate behavior during the class period are recorded against that team. At the end of the period, the team with the least number of disruptions earns an extra 5 or 10 minutes of free time while the other team is required to continue working on math problems. A further contingency was established so that if both teams had one or no disruptions that period, they both earned the free time. During the social science period, the class was divided into two groups that identically matched the Good Behavior Game teams of the math period; however neither teacher knew this, nor did the students indicate they were aware of it on a postexperiment questionnaire. In the social science period, one team was taught a course in operant behavior and self-management while the second team participated in a very interesting course in general psychology including such topics as perception, hypnosis, problem solving, how to study, and parapsychology.

The hypothesis was that if the students in the self-management class understood the procedures, they would use them to reduce their frequency of disruptions in the Good Behavior Game while the frequency of disruptions of the students in the general psychology class would remain unchanged. This was exactly what happened. As the students were taught to use the behavioral procedures to control their own responses, their rate of disruptions dropped to near zero. After the completion of the experiment, the students were asked if they realized there was a connection between the self-management class and the Good Behavior Game and if they had used any of the procedures they had learned in any other class to help in the Good Behavior Game. None of the students reported recognizing that the two classes were part of the same experiment, but over half reported trying to use some self-management skill during the math class. Interestingly, two students had gotten together with a third student who was consistently disruptive in math to help him control himself. The results on the other dependent measures also supported the interpretation that the students had learned some important self-management skills in the course (see Figure 3-1).

We were very encouraged and excited about these results. They suggested that it was possible to teach a general set of skills that adolescents would use in situations other than the training program itself. Based on this preliminary success, an extensive formal course in self-management was proposed to be added to the middle school curriculum. Unfortunately, we were unable to articulate a rationale for the course that school systems found compelling. The course was proposed to several school districts on a no-cost experimental basis and none was willing to accept it. There were undoubtedly a variety of reasons for this failure, but fundamentally, behaviorism simply is not very popular with educators. Further, there was still considerable residual controversy over Skinner's (1971) *Beyond Freedom and Dignity*, and many administrators recognized possible trouble if they supported implementing a Skinnerian program in their school. As a consequence, the self-management program was put on the back burner for a while.

Working with Delinquents and High School Dropouts

The next opportunity to work on the self-management project came through some contacts with a juvenile court that was overburdened with problem adolescents and looking for help. Under those circumstances, the behavioral orientation of the program was less of a problem. So the next study (Gross *et al.*, 1980) involved working with delinquent and predelinquent youths referred to the program by the court. This change in population led to a shift in emphasis in order to focus on helping adolescents who were already in trouble. Nonetheless, the basic strategy

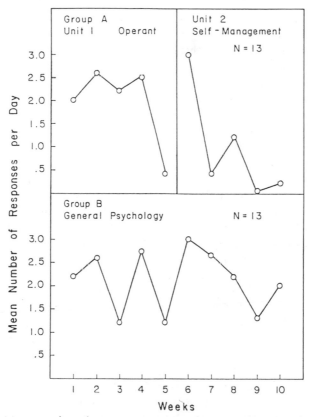

FIGURE 3-1. Mean number of target responses per day emitted by Group A and Group B during the 10 weeks of the Good Behavior Game. From *The Development and Experimental Validation of a Course in Self-Management for Sixth Graders* by J. Niemann and T. A. Brigham (1976, May). Paper presented at the meeting of the Association for Behavior Analysis, Milwaukee. Reprinted by permission.

remained the same: Teach basic concepts and procedures before attempting to deal with specific problem behaviors.

In the interim, some of the lessons had been written out, so the program now included 10 readings, in addition to the study guides. This made it possible to modify the instructional procedures from a lecture–discussion format to more of a discussion–demonstration one. This change was accomplished by assigning a reading and requiring that the student bring a completed study guide to the next class session. The elimination of the lectures made it possible to cover the material in greater detail. A related change in format was an increase in the length of the program sessions to 1½ to 2 hours. This increase was necessary for efficient scheduling because the program was no longer school based; rather, the adolescents came to the Self-Control Unit for their meetings once or twice a week.

A second major instructional change was the increased importance and complexity of the adolescents' self-management projects. Because these youths were already in trouble with the courts and generally had poor relations with their parents, they were asked to select behaviors to change that would have a significant impact on some important problem area. More-extensive baselines were collected, and the intervention results were evaluated by both self-report and significant other data. A further important addition to the program was a section on contracting and negotiation as a method of resolving family conflicts. Each adolescent and his/her parents were required to negotiate a contract and then evaluate its effects on a particular family problem.

Likewise, the evaluation of the program had to be modified. A multiple-baseline across-groups design was used to assess program impact on parent and teacher ratings of the youths' behavior and the frequency of their delinquent acts. Again, the results were quite promising, with increased positive ratings and a decrease in problem behavior being correlated with program participation. At a 6-month follow-up assessment, none of the youths had had further difficulties with the courts. The program's effects with delinquent and predelinquent youth have been clinically replicated a number of times, most recently by de Armas, Kern, and Brigham (1986).

Various aspects of self-management skills training were further explored in several studies with diverse groups. The most notable of these (Brigham, Contreras, Handel, & Castillo, 1983) evaluated the impact of self-management training on the job-getting skills and successes of high school dropouts who were participating in a federally supported graduate equivalency diploma (GED) program. Those students who took part in a self-management course were far more successful at acquiring jobs at a 6-month follow-up than those who participated in the standard job skills course ($\chi^2 = 11.6$, $p < .001$).

The next opportunity to work in a public school system occurred as a function of personal contacts with a middle school principal whose school was experiencing major discipline problems. In an effort to deal with classroom disruptions, the school had previously instituted a schoolwide assertive discipline program (Canter & Canter, 1976). This program consisted of training for teachers on how to discipline, as well as reward, appropriate behavior and a set of school rules. Violation of these rules resulted in after-school detention. Although the program had had a generally positive effect on overall school discipline problems, there remained a clear subpopulation of students who continued to have great difficulties. The Self-Control Unit was invited to design and implement a program to assist these students. With the school's endorsement, it was possible to obtain Department of Education funding to support this effort.

Effects of Self-Management Training on Disruptive Behaviors

The ensuing experiments (Brigham, Hopper, Hill, de Armas, & Newsom, 1985) represent the most extensive analysis of the self-management program to date, and therefore are presented in greater detail. The formal implementation and evaluation of the program extended over a 3-year period. The school system, however, voted to use its own funds to support the program after the grant terminated, and the school continues to provide information on the program's operation.

During the grant period, 103 6th-, 7th-, and 8th-grade students participated to some degree in the project; and it was possible to compile complete data sets on 79 of those students. The majority of these students would be characterized as acting out, impulsive, or immature. None of these adjectives represent an adequate behavioral definition, but each conveys the idea of a student who talks back to teachers, pokes another kid at the wrong time, runs and yells in the halls, or hands in assignments late if at all. Although this is not a scientific description, it is certainly one that most teachers, counselors, and administrators recognize.

The majority of the 79 students were male (70), and they were approximately evenly distributed among the 6th (28), 7th (25), and 8th (26) grades. In general, they also tended to be academically weak students, with only 16 doing B or above work before participating in the class. The largest group of students in the program were characterized by their teachers as being immature or impulsive, and their infractions tended to fall into the categories of speaking without permission, being out of seat, and other minor classroom disruptions. A sizeable minority (14) of the participants, while breaking the same sorts of rules, also displayed more serious behavior problems. These students were characterized by the school's administrators and counselors as calculated rule breakers. Their responses of lying, stealing, physically threatening, and so on, were more serious but generally emitted in such a way as to avoid major consequences. Finally, 6 students, in addition to having difficulties with the school rules, were truants, often missing a week of school at a time.

The staff of the self-management class for the 3-year project consisted of a half-time certificated teacher who was in charge of administering the program and conducting the class, as well as a full-time aide. Both instructors were taught the basics of behavioral analysis and self-management. In addition, researchers met with the instructors on a regular biweekly basis, for approximately 3 hours, to review concepts and procedures, to go over the operation of the self-management program, and to discuss any special student problems.

The instructor of the self-management class carefully recorded and monitored the number of detentions each student received. When a student received the 8th detention within one quarter, a letter was sent home to the parents or guardians. In addition to the letter, the student met with the vice principal. Students were told that reaching the 12th-detention criterion would qualify them for the self-management class.

When the student qualified for the class, he/she met with the instructor to discuss the class. The positive aspects of the program were emphasized. Students were urged to use the class as an opportunity to learn how to avoid getting detentions and to get along better in school. Throughout the course of the program, the instructor made the class enjoyable as well as informative for the students.

When the detention criterion was met, a group of four to six students was formed. Then, the students began the self-management course, which consisted of 1-hour classes 3 days a week. The classes met after school for 6 weeks. In addition, each student was required to successfully complete a self-management project. If it was not finished after 6 weeks, the student continued to meet individually with the instructor until it was completed. The longest any student continued meeting with the instructor was 3 weeks. Overall, only six students went beyond the standard length course. The first part of the course consisted of an introduction to behavior analysis. Specifically, the importance of objectively observing and measuring behavior was taught. Additionally, the principles and procedures of reinforcement, punishment, extinction, shaping, and stimulus control were taught as methods for changing behavior. The second half consisted of descriptions of contracting and negotiating, as well as applying the procedures to self-management problems. The major focus of instruction was on teaching the students how their behavior affected others. To accomplish this end, they conducted several simple experiments, with positive reinforcement and extinction to measure the impact of how changing their responses influenced other people's behavior. This notion of observing both their own behavior and others' reactions to it was emphasized throughout the program.

Once the skills were acquired, the students planned and implemented a self-management project. The self-management projects were usually very simple, but they always involved a behavioral analysis of the problem situation, a written set of specific concrete intervention procedures, and a behavioral contract with the self-management class instructor. The students were encouraged to identify a key behavior to increase (e.g., positive statements, appropriate class participation) or decrease (e.g., rule-related behavior). The objective, again, was not only to change that particular behavior but also to demonstrate to the students that they could influence how people reacted to them by changing their own behavior. As noted, students continued to participate in the class until the self-management project was completed. Role playing, modeling, study guides, and quizzes were used to teach the basic skills. The students were encouraged and assisted by the instructor to practice the skills. Most of the role-playing and modeling exercises were directed at school and interpersonal relations with peers and adults. Each unit in the manual is accompanied by a study guide that was completed independently by each student. When students completed each unit, they were quizzed about the material. Students had to score 80% or better on each unit quiz before being allowed to go on to the next unit. If students did not meet the criterion, they restudied the material and took the quiz again.

In addition to the statistical analyses of pre and post data, whenever possible, a multiple-baseline approach to the implementation of the self-management training was used. Over the 3-year period of the project, nine such analyses of the implementation of the training were completed. These quasi-multiple-baseline analyses were conducted by delaying the initiation of the self-management training for one group until a second group of students had qualified for the program. There would then be two groups of students with unacceptably high rates of detentions who had not yet received self-management training. The second group of students then formed a quasi-control group, which started the self-management class 2 or 4 weeks after the first.

One such quasi-experiment occurred when nine students had met the criterion for participation. They were randomly divided into two groups. During the week the first group began class, four more students qualified, and the principal agreed to delay the beginning of their class by approximately 4 weeks. Thus, three groups were formed at nearly the same time, with their self-management classes beginning at 2-week intervals. Although not a true three-group multiple-baseline design, the arrangement does provide an indication of the correspondence between the onset of the training and changes in student behavior.

Because detentions were the primary consequence of the assertive discipline program, they were selected to be the major dependent variable in the study as well. To ensure that detentions were being assigned consistently, both the vice principal and the self-management class instructor periodically observed every teacher. The teachers were then given feedback on their use of the discipline program and their assignment of detentions. Although the observation and feedback were not conducted as reliability checks, they served some of the same functions in maintaining the equivalence of detentions as a measurement unit across time and classrooms.

Teachers recorded the detentions earned by each student enrolled in their classes and turned in that record daily to the self-management class instructor. Each detention given represented one rule violation. The number of detentions received by each student prior to, during, and after class participation was collected and recorded in each student's individual file. In addition, at the end of the day, all detentions were recorded in the school's master file by student, date, and teacher assigning the detention. Finally, all detention slips were retained and filed by week. Before the detention records were analyzed, they were checked against the master file, and any discrepancies were resolved by consulting the original detention slip.

Other dependent measures used in the study were as follows:

Teacher Behavior Rating Scale (Gross *et al.*, 1980). The teacher scale consisted of 10 questions covering pertinent school behavior; for example, "He/she is often late for class." Each student's teacher filled out the form when the student had reached eight detentions in a single quarter and after the student's participation in the self-management class. The 5-point scale ranged from "very characteristic" to "very unlike" the student in question.

Behavior Principles Test. This instrument tested the student's knowledge of basic operant principles and procedures. There were two forms, each consisting of matching, fill-in-the-blank, and short-answer questions, for a total of 33 points. Some groups received Form I first; others were given Form II as a pretest. There were no statistical differences between the results of the two forms, so the results are grouped for the pre–post analysis.

What Would You Do If? This was a 10-item multiple-choice instrument that presented the student with a problem situation and four alternate ways of behaving. One alternative embodied a procedure based on a self-management principle and was considered the correct answer.

Self-Management Project. All students were required to complete one self-management project. The students had to plan, implement, and analyze their own behavior-change project. A written report consisting of the behavior selected by the student, the plan, data collected, and analysis was required.

Student Evaluation Scale. At the completion of the course the students were given the opportunity to evaluate the class. This test was an 11-item instrument with a 7-point scale modeled after the Teaching Family approach to consumer evaluation (Wolf, 1978). The survey covered staff and program concerns, fairness, and effectiveness.

Program effects were evaluated by three distinct groups of data. The first set of data examined was frequency of student detentions in the pre–post and in the follow-up. Related to these data are the individual patterns of detentions observed in the multiple-baseline study, which are presented separately. Finally, the pre–post results from the questionnaires, scales, and tests measuring different facets of student behavior were statistically analyzed.

For examination of the overall results of the program, the frequency of detentions displayed by all of the participants per quarter (pre- and postclass participation) were statistically analyzed. The differences observed were significant at the .05 level for the 2nd year and at the .01 level for the next 2 years. Table 3-1 shows that the students had preclass detention frequencies above the 12-per-quarter criterion, but their postclass mean frequency dropped below that level.

To test for the homogeneity, or consistency across students, of the observed effect on detentions, chi-square analyses were done on the direction of change in the frequency of detention postclass participation. The observed frequencies of change were compared to a hypothetical zero-sum model in which it was predicted that equal numbers of students would fall into the decreased, increased, and no-change categories. The pattern of results for each school year produced χ^2s that were significant at the .001 level [$\chi^2(2, N = 34) = 29.8, p < .001; \chi^2(2, N = 21) = 32.66, p < .001; \chi^2(2, N = 24) = 22.5, p < .001$].

TABLE 3-1. Statistical Analyses of Frequencies of Detentions per Quarter before (Pre) and after (Post) Self-Management Class Participation

Year	Number of students	Pre $\bar{X}$	Post $\bar{X}$	df	t	p
1979–1980	34	15.1	10.2	33	2.3	.05
1980–1981	21	12.8	7.6	20	3.3	.01
1981–1982	24	16.1	9.2	23	3.8	.01

Note. t-test used for correlated data.

TABLE 3-2. Statistical Analyses of Follow-Up Frequencies of Detentions per Year by Students Who Participated in the Self-Management Class

Class	1979–1980 $\bar{X}$	1980–1981 $\bar{X}$	1981–1982 $\bar{X}$	df	t	p
1979–1980	43	29.6		18	5.469	.001
1980–1981		38.6	27.6	17	2.8	.01

Note. t-test used for correlated data.

Similar statistical analyses were done on the follow-up detention frequencies of students who participated in the Class 1 year and remained in the school the next. The follow-up data indicate that the majority of students continued to display a significantly lower frequency of detentions in the year after their participation in the self-management class. These data and the t-test analyses are presented in Table 3-2. Chi-squares were again computed on the direction of change and indicated a significant number of students had decreased their frequency of detentions [1979–1980: $\chi^2(2, N = 19) = 17.5, p < .001$; 1980–1981: $\chi^2(2, N = 18) = 16.34, p < .01$].

The frequency of detentions received by the 13 students who participated in the quasi-multiple-baseline study are presented in Figure 3-2. Individual data are presented rather than group means because a general pattern of results emerged in individual graphs that was obscured by group data. For instance, Student 5 is a clear example of the group of individuals (11) whose frequency of detentions remained periodically high. This student was rated by his teachers as unimproved (Teacher Behavior Rating Scale mean prescore 1.2, postscore 1.35) and continued to be considered by the staff as a problem student. On the other hand, Student 6 was one of 3 students whose frequency of detentions immediately dropped to zero at the beginning of class and essentially stayed there. The timing of the change makes it unlikely that instruction in self-management was responsible for the initial change.

The remainder of the students can be roughly grouped as displaying patterns represented by Students 1, 10, and 13 or that of Student 2. Students 1, 10, and 13 show a decline in their frequency of detentions during class with postclass levels of near zero. These students received an occasional detention after class participation, but they did not fall back into their previous pattern of receiving four or five detentions in a single week (frequently on the same day). Student 2 represents the other typical form of student behavior after participation in the class. He had a fairly high postclass frequency of detentions, but it never went over the 12-

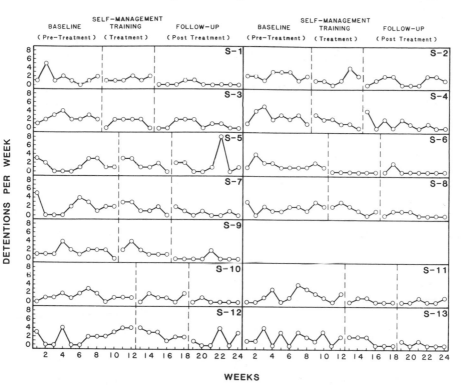

FIGURE 3-2. The number of detentions received by each student during baseline, training, and follow-up. From "A Self-Management Program for Disruptive Adolescents in the School: A Clinical Replication Analysis" by T. A. Brigham, C. Hopper, B. Hill, A. de Armas, and P. Newsom (1985). *Behavior Therapy, 16,* 99–115. Copyright 1985 by the Association for Advancement of Behavior Therapy. Reprinted by permission.

detention criterion that would have resulted in his being placed back in the class or possibly being suspended. This pattern continued to a degree the next year, when he received 20 detentions.

The statistical results of the pre–post comparison for the Teacher Behavior Rating Scale were positive [pre $\overline{X}$ 2.78, post $\overline{X}$ 3.93, $t(78) = 4.6$, $p < .01$]. However, the same patterns of score changes were observed as those in the frequency of detentions. That is, the 10 students who actually increased in detention frequency also scored the same or worse on the Teacher Behavior Rating Scale. Similarly, the low-frequency group scored much better, and the group represented by Student 2 received a wide range of scores on the different items and from different teachers.

As would be predicted, the scores on the two measures of self-management and behavior analysis concepts significantly improved from the pre- to postclass administrations. As presented in Table 3-3, before participation, students selected the self-management alternative on the multiple-choice "What Would You Do If?" questionnaire about 3 or 4 times out of the 10 questions (highest score = 5, lowest = 0). After the participation in the course, the self-management alternative was selected on approximately 8 out of the 10 questions. There was, however, an important variation in student performance on this instrument. A sub-group of 11 students scored at or below 50% on the posttest; of these, 8 either increased or displayed no change in their frequency of detentions after class participation. A chi-square comparison of students who score above 50% with those scoring 50% or below related to their patterns of postclass detentions showed a significant difference between the two groups $[\chi^2(1, N = 79) = 9.49, p < .01]$.

Because the format of the Behavior Principles Test required fairly technical answers, the preclass scores were very low, with the majority of the students receiving a zero. Again, after participation, the students did significantly better, with most scoring in the 80–90% range.

The self-management projects were very informally evaluated. The criteria were whether the student selected and behaviorally defined a response to work on, wrote an acceptable plan for changing the response, and made an "honest effort" to carry out the procedures. These judgments were all made by the self-management class instructor. The major-

TABLE 3-3. Statistical Comparison of Student Scores on the "What Would You Do If?" Questionnaire and the Behavior Principles Test before (Pre) and after (Post) Self-Management Class Participation

Year	Participants	Pre $\bar{X}$	Post $\bar{X}$	df	t	p
1979–1980						
What Would You Do If?	34	35.3	73.5	33	−5.6	.001
Behavior Principles Test	34	4.82	87.8	33	−37.3	.0001
1980–1981						
What Would You Do If?	21	37.1	84.3	20	−8.22	.001
Behavior Principles Test	21	4.52	90.52	20	−54.81	.0001
1981–1982						
What Would You Do If?	24	36.25	82.5	23	−8.1	.001
Behavior Principles Test	24	4.54	90		−50.9	.0001

Note. *t*-test used for correlated data.

ity of the projects were concerned with responses that had consistently led to detentions for the student. All 79 of the students who completed the program also completed a self-management project. Some students went well beyond the minimum requirements and conducted quite sophisticated projects in conjunction with the instructor. In those instances, the students used essentially the same procedures but applied them to more than one behavior, according to a multiple-baseline design. Over the 3 years of the program, 10 students, in consultation with the teacher, conducted projects of this quality. Of those students, 6 achieved detention frequencies of near zero and none increased over their baseline frequencies.

Finally, the course was rated very highly by the majority of students. The mean score on each item was over 6 out of a possible 7, and the median for each item was 6. There was an occasional score of 4 or below on single items, and a minority group of students (five) gave the course a neutral (4) or negative rating (less than 4). No statistical analyses of these results were done, but the overall pattern of ratings suggested that the students found the self-management class to be a positive experience.

As a whole, the results of the 3 years of program development suggest that the self-management training procedures were effective in teaching the majority of students how to reduce their frequency of detentions. There were clear changes in the number of detentions received by the students, as indicated by both the t-test and chi-square analyses. The magnitude of the changes in detention frequency was not only statistically significant, but in the majority of cases, it was of social significance as well. Some students displayed dramatically reduced frequencies of detentions following participation, others a moderate reduction, and, not unexpectedly, some actually increased. Those students showing a moderate reduction are of special interest because the change, while not great, in most instances moved the student from the "problem" category to the "acceptable." That is, teachers can and will work with a student who "screws up" occasionally as long as he/she knows when to stop. A representative comment from a teacher concerning such a student after self-management training was, "He no longer goes off the deep end."

Similarly, the students who increased in detentions also provide valuable information about the limitations of the approach taken here. The disruptive behavior of these students was generally more severe. Further, the students themselves were frequently in trouble with the legal authorities. The program was operated in a strictly instructional fashion. No contingencies were manipulated outside the self-management class.

These results suggest that a totally instructional program is not sufficient
for students characterized as predelinquent, and the programs recently
run with such youths (e.g., de Armas *et al.*, 1986) have been modified to
deal with this concern.

Some Theoretical Problems and Experimental Replications

Limitations on the applicability of the instructional self-management
approach taken in the present research are further illustrated by some
post hoc analyses comparing successful students with those who either
failed to improve or were unable to maintain their improved behavior
post class participation. As noted by Barlow *et al.* (1984), the careful post
hoc examination of failures can often provide considerable information
about the generality of a program or procedure. In the present case, it
was found that the posttest performance on the "What Would You Do
If?" questionnaire was related to postclass detention frequencies, with
students who scored 50% or below displaying significantly different
patterns of detentions from those who scored above 50%. This distinction
probably reflects a variety of factors, but it is likely that the students'
general academic skills played an important role here. The teacher com-
mented on occasion that the materials were simply too hard for some of
the students. The teacher was able to assist such students with concrete
techniques and answers in class, but the acquisition of general skills or
rules reflected in the "What Would You Do If?" instrument did not
consistently occur. Thus, the academically based and concept-oriented
approach used in this study appears to have been less effective. Recently,
Kern and de Armas (1986) have developed some simplified procedures
for working with educationally disadvantaged students, which appear
very promising.

Another student characteristic, at least partially related to postclass
detention frequencies, was the level of the students' preclass behavior
problems. However, because systematic psychometric testing is not done
in the school district, this is a very speculative conclusion with no
standard testing data to support it. As indicated earlier, the administra-
tive staff and the self-management class teacher identified 20 of the 79
students as having more severe behavior problems. An examination of
these students' records showed that 12 decreased in detentions, 4 increased, and 4 stayed the same. This pattern of postclass detentions was
found to be significantly different from that of the remaining 59 students
$[\chi^2(2, N = 79) = 8.02, p < .05]$. In addition, only 7 changed in ways that
could be called of applied or social significance (a decrease of 5 deten-

tions per quarter and improved scores on the teacher rating scale). Although these results are somewhat disappointing, again they are not surprising because systematic positive contingencies were not programmed outside the self-management class for increased positive behaviors. This lack of systematic positive contingencies now appears to have been an error because several of these students who did make positive changes in their behavior mentioned how important it had been to them that a teacher or principal had praised their new attitude toward school. It is possible that the addition of systematic positive contingencies to the program would make it more effective with students displaying more serious behavior problems, while enhancing program effects with other students.

In addition to positive changes in the frequency of detentions for the majority of students, most students also improved in their understanding of behavioral principles, as evidenced by their ability to select a self-management response on the "What Would You Do If?" questionnaire and their general classroom performance, as rated by their teachers. Also, some students displayed very sophisticated understanding of behavior analysis concepts and procedures by conducting multicomponent self-management projects. This level of complexity was not required in the program, and it reflects the students' interest in the material. Such interest by students required to participate in the class suggests that self-management and behavior analysis may be appealing to adolescents in general.

A number of questions remained after the completion of this project concerning what the essential program features were and whether the results could be replicated at other sites. The major theoretical issue was the possible confounding of punishment effects with the self-management training. Because program participation occurred as a direct consequence of excessive rule violations, the mandatory attendance at 18 hours of self-management training could be viewed as a punishment contingency. Although the immediate and frequent assignment of after-school detention had had little apparent impact on the students' behavior, the assignment of the equivalent (from some perspectives) of 18 hours of detention at one time may have been sufficiently aversive to suppress the inappropriate responses in and of itself. The observed gradual rather than immediate change in the behavior of most students and the very positive students ratings of the program argue against this interpretation. Nonetheless, a punishment explanation remained a plausible if not compelling alternative.

Likewise, the program at this school was blessed with an exceptionally fine staff. The overall positive results could have been due to the general enthusiasm, dedication, and interpersonal skills of these people rather than any particular feature of the self-management program per se. Finally, the results may have been a function of some form of interaction between the characteristics of this particular school and the program. Clearly, the program needed to be replicated in a different school.

In actuality, the materials and procedures were being implemented in other schools as a function of the need for alternative approaches to discipline problems. These efforts, however, were being operated by the schools themselves as counseling services with little or no concern with scientific data collection or evaluation. So, while the reports on these efforts were quite positive, they did not represent an adequate replication. For those reasons, a systematic replication under the direction of Dr. Armando de Armas was conducted in a second nearby school system.

This middle school was of similar size to the first, and it also used a discipline system based on schoolwide rules and after-school detentions for their violation, making the same major dependent variable common to both sites. The main objective difference between the two schools was in their student populations. Students in the first school came from working-class families, while those in the second were predominantly from professional and business families.

In implementing self-management skills training at the second school, two major procedural changes were made by design. First, participation in the program was voluntary. The school's vice principal developed a list of potential participants based primarily on their frequency of detentions. These students and their parents were contacted, and the program was described to them in glowing terms. When asked if they would like to volunteer, not unexpectedly, approximately a third declined. Obviously, this self-selection introduced a different potential confounding variable—that the students who volunteered were in other ways different from those who chose not to. Nevertheless, it was felt that the most important concern in this study was to eliminate the possible punishment interpretation of the first study. The second modification was the use of graduate students as the course instructors. The objective here was to examine the role of the instructor; the change had the desired effect of producing four different sections with different instructors in each.

Unfortunately, using graduate students as teachers had the much less desirable effect of making the program an "experiment" and not part of the school's regular ecology. The separation of the self-management program from the school's regular activities resulted in very poor cooperation by faculty and staff. To them, it was not "our" effort to help "our" students rather it was "theirs"—the outsiders. As a consequence, the faculty had little personal interest in or commitment to the program and, not surprisingly, most of the extensive and methodologically sophisticated evaluation procedures failed because of a general lack of cooperation.

Ironically, this problem is predictable from a behavior analysis position, but somehow we managed to ignore it in designing the study. Do not make the same mistake. The necessity of fitting a program into its environmental setting is so important, it should be considered a law. Irrespective of some absolute assessment of the quality of a program's materials and procedures, its impact in a setting will be directly affected by the degree to which it is incorporated into the system already in place.

Despite these difficulties, it was possible to collect the detention data. These data are presented in Figure 3-3. Although initially there were four groups, the results for the groups beginning at the same times in the multiple-baseline design were combined for ease of presentation

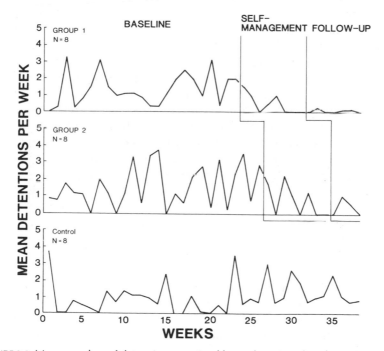

FIGURE 3-3. Mean number of detentions received by each group of students per week during baseline, training, and follow-up.

and because there were no significant differences among them. In addition, because participation was voluntary, not unexpectedly, several students dropped out. All things considered, however, the dropout rate of one third is quite modest and indicates that the students generally enjoyed the program.

In purely scientific terms, what can be said about these results is very limited. Clearly, because of incomplete data and some methodological problems, the study cannot stand on its own. Nonetheless, within the context of earlier and subsequent experiments, it does suggest that the positive results associated with the self-management training program in previous experiments were not due to punishment effects or the skills of a specific instructor.

Teaching Self-Management as an Introductory Science Course

As previously noted, early in the research it was decided to base the program on a natural science approach to human behavior, and the instructional procedures on the introductory laboratory science course. In every study, the students' mastery of the concepts and procedures of behavior analysis and science in general has been assessed. The results suggest that the students do learn a systematic and scientifically sound method for understanding their world and what is happening to them from the program. The scientific outlook aspects of the program were examined in a study (Wood & Brigham, 1987) in which self-management was taught not as a "counseling" program but as an introductory science course.

In this experiment, students in a regularly scheduled elective program were taught a 7-week section on self-management. The course was a standard part of the curriculum in which the students met 5 days a week for 55-minute periods. Thus in this study, the student population was a general sample of the 8th grade who voluntarily enrolled in the course based on title and description rather than a set of students who had gotten into trouble and were forced to attend. At the same time, all of the participating students were also enrolled in the school system's required introductory science course that focused on earth science.

At the beginning of the school year all students were pretested with the Test of Integrated Science Processes (Dillashaw & Okey, 1980), a standardized and widely recognized test of junior high and high school students' understanding of basic science processes. The students were then posttested after completing the self-management elective with the exception of the group who were scheduled to receive the elective last. These students were tested for the second time simultaneously with the posttest for the self-management Phase 3 group. Although they subsequently also received the self-management course, at this point their performance could be used as a standard (control) for improvement in science knowledge, based solely on instruction in the regular course.

The major results of the study are presented in Figure 3-4. A variety of statistical analyses demonstrated that the students gained significantly more knowledge of science processes as a function of instruction in self-management rather than in their required science course. Further, the way the testing was conducted made it possible to demonstrate clearly that the improvement in performance was correlated with the time spent in the self-management class. (For greater details on this data analysis, see Wood & Brigham, 1987.)

A final set of studies using the self-management program were conducted by Gross and his associates (Gross, 1982; Gross, Magalnick, & Richardson, 1985). These studies are important for two reasons. First, they involved an adolescent population that frequently displays many adjustment difficulties: diabetics and their families. Second, I was not

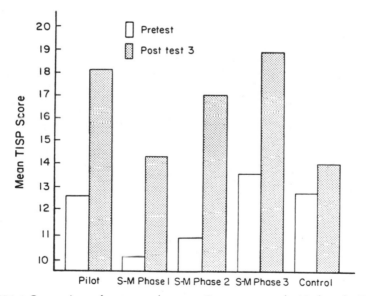

FIGURE 3-4. Comparison of pretest and posttest 3 mean scores obtained on the Test of Integrated Science Processes (TISP; Dillashaw & Okey, 1980; Tobin & Capie, 1982) by students in various group conditions. From "Psychology as a First Course in Science for Eighth Graders" by B. Wood and T. A. Brigham (1987). *Psychology in the Schools, 24*, 1–10. Reprinted by permission.

involved in designing or conducting either of these studies. Nonetheless, the investigators adopted the same general strategy of first teaching basic behavior analysis concepts and procedures before dealing with such problems as medical compliance and family conflicts. Problems such as those then became the focus of the self-management projects. The results of these studies are consistent with those previously reported. While not uniformly successful with every diabetic adolescent, the overall pattern of results were quite positive. For instance, after self-management training, Gross *et al.* (1985) found a drop to near zero in family conflicts related to medical compliance that was maintained at a 6-month follow-up.

To summarize, the results of the research conducted on the self-management skills training program to this point suggest that the basic materials and procedures can be effectively used to deal with a variety of adolescent difficulties. The program provides the adolescent with a scientifically sound behavior analysis system to understand and change what is happening in his/her life. The evidence also indicates that the youths will use the system to deal with problems other than those specifically trained and will continue to use the program after the training period has ended.

4

Teaching Self-Management Skills: Some General Observations and Programmatic Suggestions

A child who hears something
    will forget it
A child who sees something
    will remember it
A child who does something
    has knowledge
          —Chinese Proverb

An Instructional Philosophy

Substituting student for child in this proverb produces a good statement of the educational philosophy embodied in the self-management training program. The program is designed so that the student can learn concepts and procedures by doing—that is, making many responses. The role of the instructor is to facilitate learning by providing appropriate cues, guidance, and feedback. A learning experience involves an interaction between the student (his/her responses) and the instructor (parent, teacher, sibling, friend, or the physical environment). For learning to progress at a high rate, the student needs a skilled instructor who provides immediate feedback, prompts lots of responses, and guides the responses so that the student learns the concept (gets the idea) and not just a fragmented set of responses. The students' workbook, *Managing Everyday Problems*, provides the stimuli for student responses, but it is the instructor who must make the course work. During the development of the workbook, there were reasons put forth to produce it in the form of a popular self-help manual. Applied research in education and the analysis of basic learning processes suggests, however, that while a self-help manual would make a lot of money, it would not teach very much. Because the objective is to teach adolescents some concepts and procedures that can be very helpful to them, it is necessary to enlist the assistance of individuals such as yourselves. This instructor's manual is designed to present both a rationale and a set of instructional activities for each major component of a unit. It is hoped that the instructor will play an active role not only in teaching the class but also in contributing to the content and procedures of the class. As you review the materials and teach the class, different ideas and procedures will occur to you. If you try them out and they work, let us know. The program as you are reading it is not set in stone. We anticipate improving it and hope that you will be able to collaborate in the process.

The basic approach taken in *Managing Everyday Problems* can be generally labeled "behavior analysis." Behavior analysis focuses on behavior–environment interactions and how these can be changed to influence future behaviors. The *Journal of Applied Behavior Analysis* provides many excellent examples of how these procedures have been used to solve a variety of educational problems and improve students' academic performance. If you are unfamiliar with the behavior analysis approach, there are a number of excellent introductory texts available. A pair of widely available volumes are L. Keith Miller's *Principles of Everyday Behavior Analysis* (1980) and Howard Rachlin's *Introduction to Modern Behaviorism* (1970). Reviewing texts such as these will give you a better understanding of the ideas presènted in the workbook.

In addition to the psychological ideas developed in the program, we are attempting to teach the basic concepts of science. The general approach to the analysis, interpretation, and modification (prediction) of phenomena found in science is also a good model for examining our everyday world. The ideas and methods of science are related by examples to psychological research and procedures. In this manner the students have an opportunity to learn how science operates while learning important concepts about their own behavior.

We have found that the best format for the course is to have the students read the unit and complete the study guide before class discussion. The class can then review the study guide together and discuss the main concepts. The instructor should try to get the students to give additional examples and/or discuss the workbook's examples in detail. In discussing the examples, if you can have the students act out or role play, they respond better to the main aspects of the situation. For the exercises and experiments, the procedures should be reviewed very carefully, and you should ask the student questions about procedural details. It is also helpful to rehearse the procedures in class before the students try any experiment on their own. The instructor's manual contains a variety of suggestions on how to teach the major concepts and procedures.

The instructor's manual parallels the students' workbook. The instructor should first read the students' lesson or exercise and then read the corresponding section in the instructor's manual. Finally, the students' material should be reviewed again and notes made indicating how you will deal with the main points. Although there are standard presentations for each lesson or exercise in the instructor's manual, these are essentially suggestions on the main points and how they might be taught. We do not expect each instructor to do exactly the same thing, but you should familiarize yourself with the objectives of each unit so that you can determine at the end of the period whether they have been met. The lesson guide for each unit consists of a specification of the objectives for that unit and a breakdown of the main components or concepts in the unit. A specific rationale and a set of instructional activities are given for each component. In addition, the suggested activities are things that we have done with success, but they certainly do not exhaust the possibilities. It is expected that you will find activities that work well for you. When you do, please write and tell us about them.

The overall objectives for the self-management training program are as follows:

1. Teach the basic concepts and procedures of behavior analysis so they are relevant to the student's everyday life.
2. Teach the basic concepts of science as related to experimental methods and the analysis of ideas.
3. Give the student experience conducting psychological experiments and analyzing psychological concepts.
4. Give the student experience in successfully analyzing relevant self-management problems and conducting self-management projects.

The program materials contained in the workbook and the procedural suggestions in the instructor's guide may be used in a variety of ways to produce essentially customized sequences to meet your specialized needs. For instance, the self-management materials have been used a number of times in after-school discipline programs. Because these programs usually only last 6 weeks with two or three sessions a week, it is obviously impossible to cover every lesson. In such cases, it is necessary to make some decisions about which units and exercises will be covered and what sort of instructional strategy will be used. In the following section, some of these possible courses will be outlined. But before doing so, I am going to take the opportunity to describe my idealized course. In candor, this course has never been taught in the fashion to be outlined, and given the current lack of funding for such projects, it is unlikely that it ever will be. On the other hand, perhaps one of you will be more effective than I at raising funds and convincing agencies and school boards that this is really what they should be doing for their adolescents.

The Ideal Course

My fantasy course would be taught at the sophomore level with 10 to a maximum of 15 students in each section. The class would meet five times a week for the standard 50-minute period, but not all of those sessions would be spent working as a group. In fact, much of the time, the students would be working on individualized projects or in smaller groups discussing specific points. The course would last for a full semester to give the students the time they need to fully master both the conceptual and procedural aspects of the materials. Finally, the class would be taught by a master teacher. This teacher would actually like teenagers, know when to ignore a lot of their crap but also when to be firm, remember to be positive when students are doing good work, and understand that to learn, you must try things out. Give me that course, and we will give to society young people who are going to be better adjusted, happier, more productive and know a damn sight more psychology than the average graduate student. But enough of such fantasies—on to the real programs we have run and some possible variations.

As indicated earlier, the most frequent use of the self-management program to date has been in conjunction with a school discipline system. Students are usually placed in the self-management course if they are having difficulties in school and the standard disciplinary procedures have not resulted in a reduction of those problems. The most extensive study of this use of the program is reported in the paper "A Self-management Program for Disruptive Adolescents in the School: A Clinical Replication Analysis" (Brigham et al., 1985). In this 3-year research effort, we had the students participate in a 6-week after-school class as an alternative to expulsion from school. The details of the experiment are presented elsewhere. The main point here is that the participants were students who consistently got themselves into trouble with the teachers and principals of the school. Further, we were only given 6 weeks to work with each group. Therefore the instructor had to focus her efforts on the main points of the manual and help the students design, conduct, and report a self-management project in a very short period of time. As a consequence, only 15 of the 33 units were covered. Specifically those essential units were Measurement and Definition of Behavior; Measurement and Definition of Behavior Exercise; The Experimental Method; A Psychological Experiment in Social Interaction; Operant Behavior and Consequences; Reinforcement: Positive and Negative; Punishment and Response Cost; Extinction and Time-Out from Positive Reinforcement; Shaping; Stimulus Control: Discrimination; A Laboratory Case History; Applying Behavior Analysis Skills with Others; Contracting and Negotiating; Self-Management; Designing and Conducting a Self-Management Project. In addition, the units were not always completed in the order presented in the manual. Nonetheless, the effort in those studies and all others was and will continue to be teaching the student the basic concepts and procedures of self-management, emphasizing the idea that how a person acts influences the way others react to him or her, and that you can change your own behavior, which in turn changes how other people act. The adolescent who understands those ideas will be an active problem solver and more likely to engage in appropriate behaviors to gain attention and recognition.

The standard after-school discipline-related self-management course is one way of using the program materials, but there are a number of alternative arrangements. For instance, we have used the workbook in an 8th-grade elective science course (Wood & Brigham, 1987). In this research, the course was taught not as an "adjustment" class, but rather as a "fun" introductory science class. In addition to the experiments described in the workbook, the students conducted some very elementary demonstration experiments with white rats. Contrary to expectation, all of the students were interested in working with the rats—none of the 120 students who participated reported being afraid of the rats at the end of the study. It should be noted also that properly cared for white rats do not stink. The course was 1 quarter long but met 5 days a week for 40-minute sessions. Because of the time limitations, we were able to complete only a little over half of the workbook. Although the workbook was not completed, the students in the self-management class learned significantly more basic science concepts than control students in the regular science course. Interestingly, the girls in the course performed equally as well as the boys on both the course work and the standardized measures of science concepts. Finally, the students rated the self-management class as being more enjoyable and interesting than the regular science class. Unfortunately, we were unable to measure the students' general adjustment before and after participation to see if the program would affect the students' problem-solving skills when taught as a science course. None-theless, it is quite clear that the self-management program can be taught as a regular class in the schools.

Another innovative use of the self-management program was developed by Gross and his associates (Gross, 1982; Gross et al., 1985). In these studies, adolescent diabetic children were taught general self-management skills to help them deal with the problems associated with their disorder. Adolescent diabetics and their families must modify their lifestyles so that the diabetic can normalize blood glucose levels. Diabetics must plan meals to accommodate their insulin and nutritional requirements and to compensate for changes in activity levels. The diabetic individual must also conduct daily urine and blood tests to monitor glucose and ketone levels. Such information is then used to adjust daily routines in order to maintain optimum diet, insulin, and activity balance. Failure to emit these responses can produce serious medical complications (e.g., hyperglycemia, hypoglycemia, coma). Even with these serious consequences, adolescent diabetics are frequently noncompliant, producing both medical complications and family conflict.

Rather than focusing the intervention directly on medical compliance or family problems, Gross and his colleagues first taught the adolescents the principles and procedures of behavior analysis. Instruction then moved to self-management and how the techniques of self-management could be used to deal with the problems the adolescent diabetics were having. As with the other populations of troubled adolescents, this strategy of teaching basic concepts before tackling the individual's specific problems worked very well with the diabetic adolescents and their families. Gross et al. reported a drop to near zero for family conflicts related to medical compliance that was maintained at a 6-month follow-up check. There were similar positive results regarding actual compliance. The positive results obtained in these studies suggest that the present self-management program as well as the general self-management strategy espoused here may offer a viable approach for dealing with a variety of adolescent adjustment problems.

Having just asserted the generality of the program and the approach, it is equally important to note the limitations of the program. As we indicated in an earlier paper (Brigham et al., 1985), the program was not and likely will not be effective for every student. Briefly, the limiting factors appear to be the individual's reading skills, the severity of the problems, and the lack of family or environmental support. Our school-based programs have been least successful with students displaying poor academic skills and/or students who have already had extensive contact with the juvenile courts.

Finally, the fact that it is not a cure-all was clearly demonstrated when an adolescent girl who was in the program as an adjunct to ongoing family therapy attempted suicide. Because she had completed most of the self-management course and appeared to be making progress on her project, it cannot be said that she did not know the approach. Rather, in her case, simply knowing how to do something was not enough. Our minimal indirect intervention strategy is not appropriate for cases where more aggressive treatment interventions are indicated.

Some of these difficulties can be dealt with by either running the self-management program as a component of a larger treatment intervention package or by modifying the instructional format of the program. An example of the latter strategy is a study just completed by Kern and de Armas (1986). Students in a special-education resource room program were taught self-management using the concepts and procedures presented in the students' workbook, but they did not read the workbook. Rather, the instructor led discussions based on a simplified outline written on a blackboard, cartoons, demonstrations, and role-play exercises. Although these students' general mastery of the material was not at the same level achieved in the standard programs, the authors report important positive gains in their ability to manage their own behavior and that of others.

A more likely use of the materials, however, is as a program to assist adolescents who are having adjustment problems. Those problems can range from minor behavior and academic problems in school through family disruptions to the major difficulties of the adjudicated delinquent. In designing such a program, you first need to do a behavioral analysis of the problems of the adolescents and their general living situation. For example, the analysis must consider how well the individual is doing in school, whether the adolescent is a member of a group that supports or reinforces the problem behaviors, and how good the person's family relations are. Of course, this is not an exhaustive list, and many other factors to be examined will occur to you. The main point is that this sort of analysis must be done before it is possible to design the specific self-management program.

The next step in the design of a program to meet some specific needs is to read the entire students' workbook, carefully taking notes about how particular procedures or ideas may be relevant to the adolescents' problems. The workbook itself is organized in a conceptually logical and consistent fashion, which may be totally inappropriate for some programs. Consistent with the assumption that the student must understand the concept or principle before the related procedure can be effectively used to manage behavior, the workbook first deals with basic concepts and procedures before systematically discussing their application. Thus, the workbook is divided into two parts: (I) Principles and Procedures of Behavior Analysis, and (II) Applying Behavior Analysis Skills. This undoubtedly is the way the course would be organized if you were teaching it to graduate students who are simply trying to learn the ideas and have no pressing needs for the related skills. Unfortunately, most often the adolescent will be in the class precisely because of that need. As a consequence, the program must try to balance the students' immediate needs with the instructional requirements to ensure long-term effectiveness. Most of the programs designed for troubled adolescents now begin with Units 18 (A Laboratory Case History) and 22 (Contracting and Negotiating) before covering the more general Units 1 through 11. The instructional sequence after that is determined by the specific problems of the adolescents and the time available. For the general all-purpose program, Units 19 (Applying Behavior Analysis Skills with Others) and 20 and 21 (both about improving friendship) would be covered next and then once again some basic units such as 12, 13, and 17 would be studied. In this fashion, it is possible to provide the student with both basic and practical information while maintaining interest in the material.

The Use of Consequences in the Program

After reading the students' workbook, the instructor's guide (Chapter 5) should be carefully examined. With the information gained from the behavioral analysis and the review of the instructional materials, it now should be possible to decide which units will be used in the program and in which order. Next, it is necessary to decide how the course will be taught. Somewhat paradoxically, while a major section of the program is about consequences, consequences have not been systematically used in the school-based programs. There are a number of reasons for this apparent inconsistency. The first relates to the social psychology of the schools themselves. There is a widely held view that individuals violating discipline rules should be punished. To be acceptable to the general public school community, consequences for such students must be seen as aversive or at least not as positive. Attending an after-school program on self-management is acceptable within this perspective because the student is forced to do something he/she would not voluntarily choose to do. Nonetheless, if students were then extrinsically rewarded with prizes, and so on, for learning the material, this would be seen as indirectly positively reinforcing their misbehavior.

The second rationale is more theoretical and has to do with the question of what will maintain the behaviors outside of the classroom. We have focused the instruction on using the procedures outside of the classroom to produce reinforcers. Only if the responses actually produce positive reinforcers for the students will they be used in a regular fashion to solve personal problems. Thus, it is possible that directly reinforcing learning the procedures per se could interfere with the students actually using them. Though this outcome need not be the case, if reinforcers are used in the program, they should be made contingent not only on learning the procedures but also on using them outside the classroom (this is elaborated more fully in the following section).

This strategy involves an important conceptual point. What we are trying to produce, teach, et cetera, in the program is not the answers to the study-guide questions, but analytical and procedural skills that will be used outside the classroom. Reinforcing correct responses to the study-guide questions can be an important component of a program; it is essential in work with delinquents or with special education groups. Nonetheless, the important reinforcers are those that the student produces for himself/herself outside the program. Thus the final injunction of this section is to give the students as many assignments as possible to use the procedures.

Running a Self-Sustaining Program

In the spring of 1986, a pilot study was conducted using a set of prototype procedures that may help increase the number of settings and situations in which the program could be used. A major and often fatal difficulty for any new program is funding. The early research on an experimental program is frequently supported by federal or state agencies and sometimes foundations. The transition from a research project to a widely disseminated and regularly employed program, however, is seldom funded. There seem to be two main paths to this wide acceptance. The program is either disseminated as a standard part of an established agency (e.g., school systems or community mental health centers) or by becoming an independent self-sustaining operation such as the Teaching Family Model program for treating delinquents.

Although the self-management approach is gaining wider acceptance in the schools and juvenile courts, an important group of adolescents appears not to be affected by either of these agencies. Adolescents who are having moderate adjustment problems in the family, at school, or with their peers are the center of a great deal of concern but very little action until those problems become more severe. Presently, no social agency has the specific responsibility for assisting such adolescents. Thus, at present, a program designed to work with them would have to be self-sustaining at least in the short term. A long-range possibility might be to demonstrate the effectiveness of working with these adolescents before severe problems developed so that an existing agency would change its mission to include the program.

In addition to being self-sustaining, such a program would have to appeal to the potential clients in some fashion other than "It will be good for you." The problem then is to design a program that will attract adolescents who are not forced to participate by the schools, courts, or other juvenile agency, yet it will pay for itself. The first step in this particular pilot project was to determine whether there was in fact a need for such a program in the community. Local schools, social service agencies, and private practitioners were contacted about their need for such a course, and they were asked whether they would refer adolescents if such a program became available. Because the response to both questions was yes, it was decided to proceed.

Although it would be most desirable to attract participants who volunteered for the program because they found it exciting and thought it would help them, realistically, adolescents are unlikely to do so. Therefore, in an effort to generate volunteers, participants were offered a salary based on class performance. As just noted and as no doubt confirmed by your own experience, this is a very tricky point. Why pay people to learn how to live better, happier lives?

There are many forms this basic objection can take, and a program need not involve monetary rewards or systematic reinforcers to evoke this objection from certain types of critics of social programs. The essential objection is that the person should change his/her response(s) because that is the way people should behave in the first place. When procedurally analyzed, what does this objection mean? It translates to become, "If you don't behave properly, we (the society, family, school, employer, etc.) will punish you." This assertion may seem unduly harsh; nonetheless, the injunction against the use of systematic positive contingencies to teach a particular skill is usually accompanied by contingencies that involve the delivery of aversive stimuli for the failure to emit the specific response(s). Thus, it is demanded that individuals work to avoid punishment rather than to systematically earn positive reinforcement. This analysis suggests that the objection to positive reinforcement frequently functionally turns out to be a statement for punishment. Gently explicating these relations can sometimes reduce the objections to the programmatic use of positive reinforcers.

A second set of arguments in favor of using positive reinforcement to involve adolescents in a program in which they would not ordinarily choose to participate is that the program and the use of reinforcers is transitional. Participation in the self-management program can be likened to a job training program. An individual in a job training program is paid primarily for learning job skills and only secondarily for doing the job per se. Once he/she has mastered the required skills, then the natural contingencies of the work place come into play. Similarly, when the adolescent has learned the appropriate self-management skills, it is expected that the existing contingencies of the environment will maintain the responses without the additional programmatic reinforcement procedures.

Irrespective of how the use of systematic positive reinforcers is justified, they appear to be necessary in running a noninstitution program. It is therefore crucial to remember the injunction to focus the contingencies on using the program's concepts and procedures as well as on learning them in the first place. Two further questions then follow: "What reinforcers should be used?" and "How should they be paid for?" In the pilot project, the students were simply paid differing amounts of money for completing the specified tasks. Teenagers always seem to need cash, and this was the easiest generalized reinforcer to use. Rather than having to set up a point system and stock a program store with items the students might or might not want, they are allowed to save or spend the money earned in the program, as they wish. This use of money is obviously not recommended for all adolescent groups, but in this instance, there appeared to be little danger of the funds being used for illicit activities.

Money is the most widely used positive reinforcer in our society because of its flexibility and ease of manipulation. It was decided to reinforce study-guide completion; negotiating, conducting, and reporting on a contract; and designing, conducting, and reporting on a self-management project with varying sums of money. In order to involve parents more directly in the program, the students were required to discuss each assigned unit and the study guide with a parent. Parents were asked to have the teenagers explain the answers to the study guide and then to initial the study guide after the discussion. When the youth brought the study guide to class, it was checked and a fee paid for completed and initialed ones. This procedure appeared to have a positive effect on the unit discussions. The other program tasks were similarly broken into two components that could be completed and consequated over several sessions. Most of these also involved the parents in some active role.

Again, it is important to emphasize that the monetary consequences were used to reinforce both learning and using the ideas and procedures. Because results of the pilot project compared favorably with those of the other studies, it appears that these sorts of contingencies can be used without their interfering with the main thrust of the program toward the analysis and modification of the contingencies in the youth's environment. In addition, there seemed to be some positive benefits to using money in this fashion. Certainly, attendance was very high, with only two students absent, each missing 1 of the 20 sessions and the others maintaining 100% attendance.

The problem of generating the funds for these contingencies was actually quite easy to solve. The maximum cost of the program reinforcers for each youth was calculated, added to the cost of the professional services of running the program, and that total was the fee charged for the overall program. This fee system was very carefully explained to both the parents and the adolescent, with the result that only those families who agreed with the general idea decided to participate. The design of the fee system also seemed to increase parent participation and involvement with the program's activities. Oddly enough, parents will frequently pay considerable amounts for a program to help their children and then remain aloof from its operation. Perhaps because it was made very clear that the parents were paying their youths for participating in the program as well as paying for the professionals' services, the parents became more interested in how their money was being spent. This tentative interpretation gains some support from the observation that the one parent who was by far the least involved had the program fees paid by a local social service agency. Further, while appearing somewhat cynical (it is not truly), the interpretation is consistent with the earlier analysis of the "normal" pattern of relations between parents and adolescents (if he/she wants it, they have to earn it). Whatever the explanation, the increased parent involvement is a potentially important positive side effect that warrants further investigation.

Based on this very preliminary study, the self-sustaining group approach appears to have a great deal of promise as a method for serving adolescents who are not appropriate for other programs. The reader no doubt will have noticed all of the qualifiers that have been used in the discussion of this project. At this point, there is not sufficient information available to say with any certainty whether and how this approach might consistently work. Plans are currently being developed for more systematic research projects in metropolitan areas to experimentally analyze the impact of these monetary contingencies on the adolescent's mastery and use of self-management skills. Those results will then be duly reported, but until that time, the reader is again invited to actively participate in these program development endeavors by communicating the results of their efforts to use any of these procedures.

Using the Study Guides

The first instructional activity for almost every unit will be to discuss the study-guide questions. There are two reasons for beginning with the study guides. First, it is a way of discovering whether the students have read the material. Second, the study-guide questions are about the most important concepts or procedures covered in the unit, and as a consequence, represent a form of topical outline for the unit. A major task for the instructor will be to make these discussions educationally valuable or effective.

In that regard, we have developed a number of techniques for increasing student participation in the discussion of the study-guide questions. The simplest is to divide your group into two or more teams that compete for points based on answers to the questions. Often, it is not necessary to exchange the points for other consequences because the competition among groups makes the points valuable in and of themselves. The involvement of the students in the study-guide competition can be further enhanced by allowing them to write several of their own questions to be asked of the other team. This activity occurs after the discussion of the standard study-guide questions. Another variation is to give each team a chance to try to stump the instructor with a question they write. Various bonus contingencies can be invented to keep the game interesting to the students.

If the program involves parents, it is possible to enlist their help to improve study-guide mastery. We have asked parents to review the study guide with their children. After discussing the answers, the parents initial the guides, which the students then bring to class. Parents are asked to encourage and reward their children for working on the study guides. This procedure has the added advantage of exposing the parents to the course material.

To reiterate, much of the instructional strategy used in the program is based on the assumption that the student has read and made an effort to understand the assigned unit before the class begins. Reviewing the study guide is a way of determining whether this assumption is justified. If the students are not reading the material, then much of the class time will be wasted.

Some Final Program-Management Considerations

As you will discover in the discussion of the units and the instructional activities, the program does not fit very well into a standard schedule of one unit per class session. Some units will require several meetings to cover adequately while others are designed to take very little initial class time but continue over a number of sessions. Scheduling the units and class activities is further complicated by the obvious truth—students can be unpredictable: A topic you anticipated covering in 20 minutes actually takes 45, and vice versa. Because the program is based on the objective of mastery, it is impossible to specify with much precision how long it will take to reach that criterion on a particular unit with any one group of adolescents. As a consequence, instructor flexibility is a behavioral requirement for the successful operation of this program.

Nevertheless, it is necessary to do some systematic planning and preparation, or the course will be superficial and chaotic rather than simply hectic. What we attempt to do is first to select the units to be covered, based on the characteristics of the group, and then to analyze how many sessions will be required to cover them. This estimate should be conservative. If you have additional time, it is easier to add units and activities than it is to delete them. Once the units and general time frame have been determined, I find it very useful to prepare a procedural outline in the form of a large calendar. The table displays when units will be covered (or at least begun), the major activities for each unit, and what projects will carry over from one session to the next. The grand design when attached to the office wall serves as both an outline and a prompt to have materials prepared for the next task.

Evaluating the Self-Management Training Program

In designing and implementing an applied program, generally the last thing considered is how to evaluate the impact of the intervention. This is a mistake. The analysis of program effects should come directly out of the design of that program, and further it should be an integral part of the project and not something added. If questions concerning dependent variables and their assessment are not asked early on, then it is likely that these procedures will be only tenuously related to the logic and method of the program. Too frequently, then, programs are evaluated by measuring outcomes that the actual procedures never contact. It is not surprising when such programs are judged to be failures; it is not even surprising when there is a positive change in the dependent variable, yet the analysis fails to persuasively explain why the change should have occurred.

Problem Analysis and Dependent Variables

The failure of an evaluation strategy often begins with the first step of program design: problem analysis. Questions of problem analysis and evaluation design are intimately related. What is it that the procedures must change to solve the problem? When that question is answered, the issue of what to measure is also determined. Occasionally, the answers will be obvious, and the dependent variables will fall into your lap, so to speak. For instance, frequency of detentions was both an obvious and ideal dependent measure for the school discipline research. Variations in the measure logically define the problem, in that students who receive many detentions are considered discipline problems while those receiving few or none are not. Further, because the detentions are closely tied to specific behaviors, the program procedures could be designed to have impact on that set of responses. Finally, detentions are a continuous measure, in that the event can occur and be detected throughout the course of the program, in contrast to pre–post measures of program success.

The problem analysis will seldom be as straightforward as that example, but the key is to force the analysis down to specific responses that the program procedures can contact. In one study (Harney, Brigham, & Sanders, 1986), the problem of poor academic performance by college student athletes was tackled. Many explanations have been offered for the academic failure of student athletes, from poor self-concepts to poor academic preparation, and numerous attempts have been made to improve academic performance based on those analyses, with little or no documented success. The main failure of such programs has been the failure to translate the problem analyses to specific responses that were logically related to the problem and could actually be changed by the program procedures. In contrast, the analysis in this study was focused on responses that could be measured and changed. Three sets of responses were selected and made the focus of the procedures: class attendance, class notes, and completing class assignments (papers and exams) on time. By changing these behaviors, it was possible for the first time to document important consistent increases in student grade-point averages—over half a grade point for some groups. The point here is not to praise this specific study but the method. The dependent variables must represent an analysis of the problem, not simply a restatement of the problem. Further, it must be logically possible to change them with the program procedures. If these criteria are not met, then the project will be a waste of time.

In designing a specific program to use the self-management training procedures and materials, conceptually, the self-management project itself can be used as the focus of the problem analysis. That is, what is this kid doing wrong and what can he/she do to change those responses? Again, the caution is to decide what to change and how that change will be measured as part of the program design rather than after. While primarily focusing evaluation efforts on continuous measures of specific responses, some paper-and-pencil instruments have been developed to assess program processes and implementation.

The Use of Some Paper-and-Pencil Tests

The first is the *Behavior Principles Test* (see Appendices A and B at the end of this chapter). This instrument was developed to do exactly what its title implies—test the students' knowledge of applied behavior analysis and self-management. If, after participating in the course, the student does not know more about these topics in a systematic fashion than before, then the course has not been properly taught and any observed changes in the key dependent measures could not be due to a change in knowledge of self-management procedures. Demonstrating an increase in knowledge does not, of course, logically prove that other observed changes were due to this change, but at the very least, a change in knowledge must be documented before the analysis can proceed.

There are two forms of the test that have been shown to be of equivalent difficulty. As a consequence, they can be given in either order without affecting the results. Although the pre–post administration of the Behavior Principles Test is the main method of documenting knowledge gains, it is important to attend to study-guide performance. Study guides are provided for most units, and while their main function is to identify important concepts and procedures for the students, they are also a continuous measure of student mastery. If the students are having difficulty with the study guides, it means that the program is not being properly implemented or that there is not a good fit between the instructional requirements of the program and materials and the students' academic skills. Stop immediately, find out why the students are not performing well, and correct the problem.

The second instrument is called the "*What Would You Do If?*" and was designed to measure the conceptual generalization of self-management principles to novel situations (see Appendix C at the end of this chapter). While the Behavior Principles Test checks students' concepts of specific items, such as, "Define negative reinforcement and give an example," this instrument uses scenarios and alternatives in which one answer represents a self-management analysis. The following example illustrates the strategy:

You and your mother always argue about the time at which you are supposed to be home after school.

a. Don't worry about it because she usually stops yelling after 5 or 10 minutes.

b. Be very friendly when you do get home so maybe she won't yell as much.

c. Complain to your dad to see if he can get her to stop bugging you.

d. Try to work out a compromise so that you can get home late a couple of nights.

Not unexpectedly, before the course the most frequent answer is "a" followed by "c," whereas after course participation, about 85% of the students select alternative "d." Again, improvement on this instrument does not guarantee that the adolescent will be better at dealing with his/her environment, but it does indicate that the individual has some basic understanding of self-management principles.

The final instrument developed for use with the self-management program is the *Youth Behavior Inventory* (see Appendix D at the end of this chapter). This scale is closely related to the Connors (Goyette, Connors, & Ulrich, 1978) and evolved because of the program's focus on self-management and the need to have the individual evaluate his/her own behavior. The inventory consists of a list of 29 specific responses in which the student is asked to indicate whether the response is characteristic (very much) or not characteristic (not at all) behavior. The student Youth Behavior Inventory has two main functions. The first is as a semidiagnostic instrument to identify responses that need to be modified. A careful examination sometimes can indicate a cluster of responses that may be important in the problem analysis or might suggest a focus for the individual's self-management project. As a posttest, the Youth Behavior Inventory can be used to assess the degree to which the adolescent believes these response patterns have changed. Based on the scores alone, it is not possible to assert that the individual's behavior actually has changed—that interpretation must be confirmed by other data. Nonetheless, positive changes in Youth Behavior Inventory scores have been correlated with other positive changes and may be indicative of the individual's commitment to changing his/her behavior.

As a quick and dirty way of measuring other people's evaluation of the student's change of behavior, two additional versions of the Youth Behavior Inventory were developed (see Appendices E and F at the end of this chapter). One is designed for parents and the second for peers. These forms serve essentially the same function as the student Youth Behavior Inventory. Again, the scores on these inventories are only indicative of behavioral change and not direct evidence. Although these instruments are useful for auxiliary analyses, the core of the evaluation process must be the direct measurement of change in dependent variables identified in the problem analysis.

Appendix A. Behavior Principles Test, Form A

Date _____

Name _____

Score _____

Fill in the Blanks I

1. The Cheapie Food Co-op assigned two clerks to count the number of customers they had prior to their advertising campaign. We call data collected prior to a treatment condition _____ data.
2. To find out how much time Dumb Tom spends watching TV every day, you should use the _____ method of measurement.
3. The goal of shaping is to produce an entirely new _____.
4. Mary interrupted Sally all the time, and the other girls in the group paid attention to her interruptions rather than to Sally's conversation. Sally finally talked the other girls into ignoring Mary's interruptions, and Mary's rate of interruptions decreased. What behavioral concept is exemplified by the group's ignoring Mary's interruption? _____
5. Kip always talked in class without raising his hand. The teacher finally got mad and started yelling at Kip every time he talked in the class without raising his hand. What behavioral procedure did the teacher use to increase the rate of Kip's hand raising? _____

Define These Terms

1. Negative reinforcement

2. Rate

3. Overt

4. Discrimination

5. Shaping

6. Generalization

Match the Following Terms to Their Definition

1. Graph
2. B. F. Skinner
3. Experimental condition
4. Reinforcement
5. Successive approximation

_____ a. is a process by which a psychologist increases the rate of a subject's behavior

_____ b. describes in picture form the occurrence of a behavior

_____ c. is a process by which an animal or human learns a new behavior

_____ d. an important psychologist

_____ e. is the treatment portion of an experiment

_____ f. an important professor of education

Fill in the Blanks II

1. Punishment is defined as an event that _____ a response and _____ the frequency of that response.

2. Differential reinforcement involves a situation in which there are two or more different _____; discrimination training involves a situation in which there are two or more different _____.

3. Punishment and reinforcement both refer to events that _____ a response.

4. Ms. Piano reinforced Toneless only when he sang a note within a half tone of A flat and then only when he sang A flat itself. This is an example of what behavioral process? _____

5. Stopping the occurrence of an event and observing a decrease in the rate of a response does not constitute extinction if the event that is stopped did not _____ (precede, follow) the response.

6. When a response (that had previously been reinforced in the presence of a particular stimulus) occurs in the presence of a similar stimulus, _____ has occurred.

7. _____ _____ is achieved when a response is more likely to occur in the presence of an S^D and less likely to occur in the presence of an S^Δ.

8. What are the three necessary rules you must follow in order for reinforcement procedures to be effective?

9. Define and write a brief example of positive reinforcement.

Appendix B. Behavior Principles Test, Form B

Name _____

Date _____

Score _____

Fill in the Blanks I

1. John was so out of shape that he got winded when putting on his shoes. He decided to get into shape and made out a behavior modification plan to help him in his effort. Prior to starting the plan, he counted how many times he jogged each week for 3 weeks. We call such data collected prior to a treatment condition _____ data.

2. Bugeyes Billy watches a lot of television. To find out how many shows he watches a week, we should use the _____ method of measurement.

3. To teach new behaviors, it is best to reinforce successive approximations to the target response. This procedure is also known as _____.

4. Late Lonny always is late for dinner. This gets his mom as mad as a hornet. So every time he is late, his mother goes berserk and yells and screams at him. Now Lonny seems to be late more often. What behavior procedure did Lonny's mom use if it resulted in an *increase* in Lonny's late behavior?

   _____

5. Soulful Sam had a habit of acting wild around his male friends whenever a pretty girl came around. Every time he did this, his friends laughed at his behavior. His girl friend, Wickedly Wonderful Wanda, thought this was a drag. She talked his friends into ignoring him whenever he started acting crazy around pretty girls. What behavioral concept is the group's ignoring of Sam's crazy behavior?

Match the Following Terms to Their Definition

1. Experimental condition
2. Duration
3. Overt
4. Discrimination
5. Extinction

_____ a. the treatment portion of an experiment

_____ b. behavior you can see

_____ c. knowing when it's all right to swear when you are with the guys but not your parents

_____ d. when you no longer reinforce the class clown for joking in class

_____ e. when you measure how long your brother spends on the phone every night talking to his girlfriend

Fill in the Blanks II

1. Punishment affects a behavior by _____ the frequency with which it occurs.

2. _____ increases the frequency of a response.

3. For a reinforcer to be effective, it should be delivered _____ after the behavior occurs.

4. In shaping, the first step is to identify the _____ response. Next, you need to identify the _____ approximations.

5. In differential reinforcement, we use both _____ and _____.

6. May makes jokes in class whenever the teacher calls on her and she doesn't know the answer to a question. Usually the class laughs at her jokes. One day the class stopped laughing and ignored all her jokes. What procedure was the class using? _____

7. Tim collected some baseline data, but he didn't know what to do with it. Jane told him he should make a _____ or a picture of how the data looks.

8. When we learn to tell the difference between two stimuli we say that we have learned to _____ between them.

9. In an experiment to determine whether the procedure you used was effective, you should compare the _____ data to the _____ condition data.

10. Margaret decided to teach her little sister how to count to ten. She decided to use reinforcement. So she decided that when she was around her sister and she was counting Margaret would reinforce her, using candy as the reinforcer. But, Margaret's sister never counted because she did not know how. What procedure should Margaret have used to teach her sister a new behavior of counting? _____

Short Answer

1. What is the difference between positive and negative reinforcement?
   a.
   b.
2. Give a definition and an example of extinction.
   a.
   b.
3. What are two of the problems that can occur when you try to use punishment?
   a.
   b.

Appendix C. What Would You Do If?

Number _____

Date _____

The following questions involve situations that sometimes happen in our lives. We would like you to select the alternative that you believe would be the best solution to the problem.

1. What would you do if you were getting into trouble for fighting with your sister?
   a. Leave the room immediately if a fight starts and try to be nice to her when she is not bugging you.
   b. Keep track of how often she bugs you and then show her how unfair she is.
   c. Tell your parents that it is really her fault, and they shouldn't punish you.
   d. Tell your sister that you really do want to get along with her.

2. What would you do if your teacher never paid any attention to you?
   a. Smile whenever he/she looks at you.
   b. Tell the principal.
   c. Tell your parents.
   d. Wave your hand in his/her face.

3. What would you do if you were getting an F in arithmetic because you never finished more than 2 problems per day, even though you could do 15 problems a day easily and really wanted to do more?
   a. Tell yourself that you must try harder.
   b. Ask your parents to help you by asking them to do some of the problems.
   c. Tell your teacher that you can only do 2 problems.
   d. Record how many problems you do every day and then add 1 or 2 problems to the amount you finished the day before.

4. You and your mother always argue about when you are supposed to be home from school.
   a. Don't worry because she usually stops yelling after 5 or 10 minutes.
   b. Be very friendly when you do get home, so maybe she won't yell as much.
   c. Complain to your dad to see if he can get her to stop bugging you.
   d. Try to work out a compromise so that you can get home late a couple of nights.

5. Suppose you are very bashful and shy, but you really want to get to know the girl or boy that just moved in next door. What would you do?
   a. Wave at the person when you see him/her. The next time, say "Hi." The next time go a little closer and ask "What is your name?" Continue this until you can ask more questions.
   b. Ask your mother to invite the person over to your house.
   c. Wait until some other kids are playing with the person outside on his/her bike and run into them with your bike.
   d. Wait until some other kids are playing with the person and then go joke around with them.

6. What would you do if you were afraid of all dogs, but you knew it was silly and wanted to be less afraid?
   a. Force yourself to run up to the next dog you see and pet him.

    b. Ask your mother and father to buy you a dog.

    c. Tell yourself over and over, I am not afraid of dogs.

    d. When you see a dog, ask the owner if it is friendly and then sit down and call the dog until it comes to you. Tell yourself you are not afraid and the dog is friendly.

7. You never answer any questions in class, and the teacher probably thinks you are pretty dumb. What can you do to make yourself answer a question once in awhile?

    a. At the beginning of the week give $2.00 to a classmate who will give you back $.50 each time you answer a question. Any money left at the end of the week, the classmate will get to keep.

    b. Just keep quiet and hope you will find a simple question to answer.

    c. Tell your mother about your problem and have her talk to your teacher about calling on you in class.

    d. Ask the person next to you what the answer is so that you can raise your hand and answer.

8. What do you do when a person is insulting to you most of the time and says nice things just once in awhile and you wish the person would always say nice things?

    a. Ask the person to speak nicely to you.

    b. When the person is insulting you, look away; only talk to the person when he/she talks nicely to you.

    c. Hit the person whenever he/she insults you.

    d. Tell the teacher or your parents about the insulting comments.

9. What do you do if you want to watch TV all evening instead of doing your homework that is due in the morning?

    a. Finish a part of your homework and then watch 1 half-hour of TV, then finish the rest of your homework and then watch TV until you have to go to bed.

    b. Tell your mother not to let you watch TV.

    c. Watch TV at night, then get up really early and try to finish your homework quickly.

    d. Forget about homework, watch TV, and tell your teacher that you had to go out with your parents.

10. What do you do if you want to save money for Christmas presents, but you always spend it immediately for records, clothes, or other things?

    a. Give all your money to your father to keep.

    b. Put half of the money you get each week into a bank and spend the rest. Repeat the procedure for several weeks, buying a present each time you have enough money, until you have all the presents.

c. Spend the money and ask your mother for a loan at Christmas time.

d. Save all your money in a bank until you have enough to buy all the presents you need.

Appendix D. Youth Behavior Inventory (Student)

Name _____

Date _____

On the next page, you are asked to decide how often you do the behavior described. If you do the behavior described a lot or in particular situations, then check under *very much*. If, on the other hand, the behavior is something you never (or almost never) do, place a check mark under *not at all*.

For example, if the statement "I frown a lot" is very accurate then place a check under *very much*.

	not at all	a little	a fair amount	much	very much
I frown a lot.					✓

If you think you only frown an average or medium amount, then check a *fair amount*.

	not at all	a little	a fair amount	much	very much
I frown a lot.			✓		

Finally if you seldom frown, you should place a check under *not at all*.

	not at all	a little	a fair amount	much	very much
I frown a lot.	✓				

This is a confidential questionnaire. After you complete it, the page with your name will be removed, and only the number will be used to identify your responses. In deciding how well a statement describes you, be as accurate as possible.

Thank you for your participation.

Number _____

	A not at all	B a little	C a fair amount	D much	E very much
1. I am rude to friends.					
2. I admit mistakes or errors I make.					
3. I show appreciation (e.g., saying "thank you") when someone does something for me.					
4. I interrupt adults when they are talking.					
5. I use foul language when talking to adults.					
6. I respond with an odd facial expression (e.g., disgust) when asked to do something.					
7. I pay close attention in class.					
8. I argue with friends.					
9. I listen carefully when teachers are talking.					
10. My performance in school is satisfactory or better.					
11. I tease people just to bother them.					
12. I yell, talk back, and curse when asked to do something.					
13. I get along well with friends.					
14. I disobey teachers.					
15. I talk back to adults.					
16. I fight with my brothers and/or sisters.					
17. I tell the truth when talking to adults.					
18. I offer to help teachers or other adults.					

	A not at all	B a little	C a fair amount	D much	E very much
19. I have to be yelled at by adults.					
20. I am late for appointments.					
21. I create disturbances in class by getting out of my seat, talking out of turn, or making noises.					
22. I am on time for class.					
23. I am cooperative and volunteer to do household chores (cleaning room, washing dishes).					
24. I do my homework.					
25. I get into arguments with adults.					
26. I hand in assignments on time.					
27. I quickly lose my temper.					
28. I participate in class discussions.					
29. I take things that aren't mine.					

Appendix E. Youth Behavior Inventory (Parent)

Your name _____

Name of student being rated _____

Date _____

On the next page, you are asked to decide how often your child does the behavior described. If he/she does the behavior described a lot or in particular situations, then check under *very much*. If, on the other hand, the behavior is something he/she never (or almost never) does, place a check mark under *not at all*.

For example, if the statement "He/She frowns a lot" is very accurate, then place a check under *very much*.

	not at all	a little	a fair amount	much	very much
He/She frowns a lot.					✓

If you think your child only frowns an average or medium amount, then check a *fair amount*.

	not at all	a little	a fair amount	much	very much
He/She frowns a lot.			✓		

Finally if your child seldom frowns, you should place a check under *not at all*.

	not at all	a little	a fair amount	much	very much
He/She frowns a lot.	✓				

This is a confidential questionnaire. After you complete it, the page with your name will be removed, and only the number will be used to identify your responses. In deciding how well a statement describes your child, be as accurate as possible.

Thank you for your participation.

Number _____

	A not at all	B a little	C a fair amount	D much	E very much
1. He/She is rude to friends.					
2. He/She admits mistakes or errors he/she makes.					
3. He/She shows appreciation (e.g., saying "thank you") when someone does something for him/her.					
4. He/She interrupts adults when they are talking.					
5. He/She uses foul language when talking to adults.					
6. He/She responds with an odd facial expression (e.g., disgust) when asked to do something.					
7. He/She argues with friends.					

	A not at all	B a little	C a fair amount	D much	E very much
8. His/Her performance in school is satisfactory.					
9. He/She teases people just to bother them.					
10. He/She yells, talks back, and curses when asked to do something.					
11. He/She gets along well with friends.					
12. He/She talks back to adults.					
13. He/She fights with his/her brothers and/or sisters.					
14. He/She tells the truth when talking to adults.					
15. He/She offers to help parents or other adults.					
16. He/She has to be yelled at by adults.					
17. He/She is late for appointments.					
18. He/She is cooperative and volunteers to do household chores (e.g., cleaning room, washing dishes).					
19. He/She does his/her homework.					
20. He/She gets into arguments with adults.					
21. He/She hands in assignments on time.					
22. He/She quickly loses his/her temper.					
23. He/She takes things that aren't his/hers.					

Appendix F. Youth Behavior Inventory (Peer)

Your name _____

Name of student being rated _____

Date _____

On the next page, you are asked to decide how often your classmate does the behavior described. If he/she does the behavior described a lot or in particular situations, then check under *very much*. If, on the other hand, the behavior is something he/she never (or almost never) does, place a check mark under *not at all*.

For example, if the statement "He/She frowns a lot" is very accurate, then place a check under *very much*.

	not at all	a little	a fair amount	much	very much
He/She frowns a lot.					✓

If you think your classmate only frowns an average or medium amount, then check a *fair amount*.

	not at all	a little	a fair amount	much	very much
He/She frowns a lot.			✓		

Finally if your classmate seldom frowns, you should place a check under *not at all*.

	not at all	a little	a fair amount	much	very much
He/She frowns a lot.	✓				

This is a confidential questionnaire. After you complete it, the page with your name will be removed, and only the number will be used to identify your responses. In deciding how well a statement describes your classmate, be as accurate as possible.

Thank you for your participation.

Number _____

	A not at all	B a little	C a fair amount	D much	E very much
1. He/She is rude to friends.					
2. He/She admits mistakes or errors he/she makes.					
3. He/She shows appreciation (e.g., saying "thank you") when someone does something for him/her.					
4. He/She interrupts adults when they are talking.					
5. He/She uses foul language when talking to adults.					
6. He/She responds with an odd facial expression (e.g., disgust) when asked to do something.					
7. He/She pays close attention in class.					
8. He/She argues with friends.					
9. He/She listens carefully when teachers are talking.					
10. His/Her performance in school is satisfactory or better.					
11. He/She teases people just to bother them.					
12. He/She yells, talks back, and curses when asked to do something.					
13. He/She gets along well with friends.					
14. He/She disobeys teachers.					
15. He/She talks back to adults.					
16. He/She fights with his/her brothers and/or sisters.					

	A not at all	B a little	C a fair amount	D much	E very much
17. He/She tells the truth when talking to adults.					
18. He/She offers to help teachers or other adults.					
19. He/She has to be yelled at by adults.					
20. He/She is late for appointments.					
21. He/She creates disturbances in class by getting out of his/her seat, talking out of turn, or making noises.					
22. He/She is on time for class.					
23. He/She is cooperative and volunteers to do household chores (e.g., cleaning room, washing dishes).					
24. He/She does his/her homework.					
25. He/She gets into arguments with adults.					
26. He/She hands in assignments on time.					
27. He/She quickly loses his/her temper.					
28. He/She participates in class discussions.					
29. He/She takes things that aren't his/hers.					

5

Instructor's Guide to Managing Everyday Problems

It is important to reiterate the need for preparation. I recommend first reading the relevant section in the instructor's guide, then the unit in the students' workbook, and finally return to the instructor's guide to actually plan the lesson. After you have worked with the program for awhile, such preparation will not be required. I have, however, observed advanced graduate students and counselors wilt in the face of groups of adolescents when they had not prepared. One of the difficulties of behavioral psychology is that it often sounds much easier to do than it actually is. Be obsessive about preparation.

Part I. Principles and Procedures of Behavior Analysis

Unit 1. Measurement and Definition of Behavior

Objective: Teach the students the importance of objective information in understanding issues and resolving conflicts.

BEHAVIORAL DEFINITIONS

Behavioral definitions—specifications of the response or responses to be observed—are the first step in looking at our own behavior objectively. We tend to describe our own behavior and that of others in very broad terms; such vague labels make communication and change very difficult. For instance, a student may report that he/she is having "trouble" because siblings, peers, teachers, parents, and so one, are "mean" to him/

her. We have all heard statements such as this, and there are at least two terms that need clearer specification: "trouble" and "mean." In order for a student to be able to understand and change the situation, these terms must be defined. Although it may seem cumbersome to try to be specific about terms or ideas, even such nonbehavioral psychologists as Carl Rogers and Rollo May suggest that we hide behind words and we need to examine what our statements mean.

Instructional Activities. The first step in discussing any unit will usually be to review the study guide. The review should consist of checking to see whether the students have the correct answers and whether they understand the idea. Understanding is checked by asking a student to give another example and then having the class comment on the second example. In this manner, it is possible to determine whether a person understands the concept well enough to produce a new example. A discussion of this sort will probably be new to most of your students, so you will have to make many suggestions in the first few discussions. You could give an example and ask how the example fits the idea, or you could give hints for the students so they could come up with a new example themselves. Alternatively, a number of possible examples could be given and the students asked to tell which is correct and why. Clearly, we are asking for very sophisticated responses, but such responses are not expected on the first few units. The students should be praised for trying, then more complex responses can be required as you move through the workbook.

After reviewing the study guide, have the students write a sentence about themselves or an acquaintance. Then discuss the sentences in terms of their meaning. We are not looking for deep insight here but rather to show how ambiguous everyday words can be. Suppose a student wrote a sentence such as "I am a very friendly, outgoing person" an analysis of the sentence would require the student to be more specific about "friendly" and "outgoing". The student needs to define what specific behaviors or responses make one friendly or outgoing.

This first exercise will probably be a little awkward, so do not expect too much; be positive; and have lots of prompts or examples ready.

An alternative to this exercise, or you may wish to do both, is to discuss and develop behavioral definitions for some of the following words:

Happy/unhappy	Sad	Rude
Angry	Mean	Intelligent/smart
Aggressive	Hostile	Cheerful
Friendly	Studying	Excited

METHODS OF MEASUREMENT

These are the specific techniques (frequency, duration, and outcome) that will be used in the course to collect objective information about the various situations that concern students. The importance of objective information is stressed throughout the manual. Students need to learn the methods so that their later analyses can be based on observations rather than their memory or general impressions of an event or inter-action.

Some ideas are introduced in this unit that will be treated in greater detail in later units. Specifically, the terms "baseline" and "experiment" need only be touched on briefly in your discussion of this unit.

Instructional Activities. The main task for this section will be to go over in class the two specific examples of measurement (the experiment with the rats eating and the observation of phone use). As the examples are discussed, the students should be asked how other measurement techniques could be used in both examples to produce information about eating or using the phone. How might the measurement system affect the information you get about those behaviors?

Because it is more relevant to the students' daily lives, the phone example will probably generate more discussion. The instructor can have the students make up data by asking them to write down two numbers (data) and then randomly call on them to give you the numbers. The data can then be graphed and the role of data in resolving conflicts discussed.

The following project may be used to substitute for both the behavioral definition and the measurement exercises because it involves both aspects of the unit.

BEHAVIORAL OBSERVATION EXERCISE

Divide the class into groups of three students each. Explain to the groups that they are to get together and develop behavioral definitions for the responses of smiling and gesturing. The groups are to work independently on the definitions, using the procedures described in the unit. Remind the students that the definition must be based on observable features of the behavior. Make sure that (1) they write the definitions down and (2) each member has a copy of the definitions. Next, have the students make data sheets. You will be using a measurement system that combines features of both interval and event recording, called "timed-event recording." The data sheet should have 10 1-minute intervals on it and two columns: one labeled "Smiles" and the other "Gestures."

	Smiles	Gestures
1.		
2.		
3.		
4.		
5.		
6.		
7.		
8.		
9.		
10.		

Explain that the students will be watching someone read a short story to them and that they are to place a tally mark (l) under the appropriate label whenever that person smiles or gestures. The students are to do their recording on a minute-by-minute basis so that responses occurring in the 3rd minute of the reading should be recorded on line three. You will need some way to time the reading so that the class will be aware of the interval. The easiest thing to do is to explain to the person reading the story that you will be announcing the intervals in a moderate voice while the person reads. This should not disrupt the reading, and it eliminates the need for equipment or complex timing procedures. You will require a reader though—someone who will be comfortable in the situation, such as a speech or language arts teacher. Ask the person in advance to be as expressive as possible while reading.

It should take about one period to explain the exercise and develop the behavioral definitions and a second period for the reading, calculation of the reliability, and discussion. Invite the reader to come in at the beginning of the second period, but before starting, make sure that the members of the class who are recording are *not* sitting together so that they cannot influence each other's recording. After the 10-minute reading, thank the person, then have the groups get together to calculate reliability. This is done by having the students compare their results interval by interval to discover agreements and disagreements, as per the example

	Smiles	Gestures	Smiles	Gestures
1.	II	II	I	II
2.	I	III	I	IIII
3.		II		I
4.	II	II	III	II
5.	I	III	I	III
6.	I	II	I	I

	Smiles	Gestures
1.	1 agreement and 1 disagreement	2 agreements
2.	1 agreement	3 agreements and 1 disagreement
3.		1 agreement and 1 disagreement
4.	2 agreements and 1 disagreement	2 agreements
5.	1 agreement	3 agreements
6.	1 agreement	1 agreement and 1 disagreement

$$\text{Reliability} = \frac{\text{Agreements}}{\text{Agreements} + \text{Disagreements}}$$

Smiles: $\frac{6}{8} = 75\%$

Gestures: $\frac{12}{15} = 80\%$

In research, we usually try to get 85 to 90% reliability to ensure that the results are accurate and do not reflect an observer's bias. Have the students present their reliability to the class. There should be considerable variation in reliability, with those students having the clearest behavioral definitions producing the best reliability.

Added bits of information
  • All things being equal, a rat will eat less food if its access to water is restricted.
  • The vertical axis of a graph is called the *ordinate*. The units of the behavior being observed are usually placed on the ordinate.
  • The horizontal axis is called the *abscissa* and is used to mark off time intervals (day, minutes, weeks, etc.).

Unit 2. Measurement and Definition of Behavior Exercise

Objective: Give the students practice reading, graphing, and interpreting data before they produce their own.

READING DATA AND TRANSFERRING THEM TO A GRAPH

Graphing data requires that the individual organize the information in some systematic manner. Picturing information by putting data on a graph is a very simple form of analysis. In the exercise, the main features of a study that had very clear results were selected. After completing the graph, the students should be able to see the relation between what Ruby's parents did and how often she hit her little brother.

Instructional Activities. The students should have read the unit in advance of class, but they should *not* try to construct the graph in advance. The graphing and analysis will be done in class. Hand out graph paper (preferably the type with the large squares), and ask the students to use pencils for this work. On the blackboard draw the ordinate and the abscissa. Ask the students what they are called and how they should be labeled (ordinate: vertical axis labeled "hits"; abscissa: horizontal axis labeled "days"). Proceed to do this on the blackboard, and check to see if the students successfully have done so as well. Next, read the first set of numbers, and ask a student to place them on the figure on the board. After the data are on the graph on the board, the students should put them on their own graphs. A vertical line is then drawn on the figure between Days 5 and 6. A vertical line on a graph indicates that there has been a change of conditions in the experiment. Ask the students how the condition should be labeled; the first condition should be labeled *"baseline."*
    Next, have a second student come to the board, read the second set of data, and then place them on the graph. The rest of the aforementioned procedure should then be repeated. After the second condition has

been completed, ask the students to try to do the next condition on their own. If they are successful, go ahead and have them complete the figure. If they are having difficulty, stop and go through the steps of putting the material on the board again.

Once the graph is completed, have the students *write out* their behavioral definition of hitting, and their evaluation of the program on the back of their graph papers. Next, have each student read his/her behavioral definition, and have the students compare their definitions to arrive at a single behavioral definition of hitting. They should then all write this definition on their papers.

The final exercise of the unit is to discuss the students' evaluation of the program for Ruby. There are three points to be made here: (1) the data tell us about the frequency of Ruby's hitting; (2) there is a relation between the reinforcement/time-out procedure and how often Ruby hits (hitting decreases); (3) these data do *not* tell us whether Ruby became a nice person or not. All we know is that she stopped hitting her little brother. At this point, you can talk about what it means to be a nice person (not hitting people is obviously a part, but it is not all there is to being a nice person).

Although it is still very early in the program, we have discovered that this is a good point to begin parts of the students' self-management project. Specifically, they should start collecting baseline data on the problem behavior they have decided to change. This, of course, requires the development of a behavioral definition and a measurement system. Have the students select two or three problems that are of concern, and then they should write out preliminary behavioral definitions for each. The students are asked to decide by the next class meeting which behavior they plan to change and to bring an expanded written behavioral definition of it to class. (Whenever possible, have the students write down their class assignments. At first, they may not be able to write very well, but they will improve, and they will learn much more from the assignment.)

At the beginning of the next class, you should collect the behavioral definitions and ask the students to outline how the response(s) will be measured for the next meeting. After the session, you should carefully critique the proposed behavioral definitions and make specific suggestions on how to improve them. If there are serious problems, class time may have to be scheduled to review how to write behavioral definitions; otherwise, hand them back and collect the measurement system outlines. The same process will be used to review them.

It will probably take 2 or 3 weeks, using bits and pieces of class time to work on definitions and measurement systems before everyone has an acceptable set. That timing actually works out very well; the students then collect 2 or 3 weeks of baseline data and are ready to start the intervention phase when they reach that point in the workbook.

Added bits of information
• The word "data" is plural. The singular form is "datum." These endings come from Latin, but in common practice the word datum seems to be disappearing. Consequently *data* is more and more being treated as both singular and plural, something like the word "deer." But to be absolutely correct you should say the data *are* _____.
• Because the vertical lines on a graph indicate a change in conditions, the data points on one side of the line should *not* be connected to those on the other.

Unit 3. The Experimental Method

Objective: Teach the elements of an experiment and how an experiment can be used to test an idea.

RESEARCH HYPOTHESIS (IDEA)

All experiments are tests of ideas or hypotheses. A *hypothesis* functionally (causally) relates at least two events. For example, "Eating onions produces bad breath" is a hypothesis or idea, which can be restated as "*If* you eat onions, *then* you will have bad breath." *Using experiments to test ideas is the single most important feature that distinguishes science from other fields.*

Instructional Activities. Each experiment described in this unit is a test of an idea or hypothesis. The first step in discussing this unit is to have the students determine the way that ideas suggest how things should work. Aristotle's idea that weights fall at a speed or rate in direct proportion to their weight meant that a 10-pound weight should fall 10 times faster than a 1-pound weight. Galileo clarified the implication or prediction in Aristotle's idea and tested it. Analyzing an idea is the beginning step in designing an experiment. The other two ideas in this unit are (1) bacteria cause wine to spoil, and (2) Cathy crawled because it produced attention. Each of these ideas makes a prediction.

After the students have determined the ideas and predictions of the experiments in the unit, try to have them analyze some other ideas. Even ideas that don't seem to make predictions can be analyzed in this way. A commercial says that Burger King Whoppers are better than Big Macs. The statement makes the prediction that if a neutral observer tastes a Whopper and a Big Mac, the Whopper will be selected as better tasting. Commercials are a very good source of statements to analyze. Have the students suggest statements with which they are familiar and then analyze them to see how they could be tested. *Penny Power* magazine is a good source of examples of adolescents testing commercial claims.

THE EXPERIMENT

The experiment involves manipulating or changing a variable specified in the idea or hypothesis. The essential step in the advance of science was the development of the experiment. An experiment allows the scientist to test the accuracy of his/her ideas by actually manipulating or changing some factor (independent variable) to see if the relation predicted in the idea is true or false. In this manner, the analysis (explanation) of phenomena could be based on objective information rather than opinion. *It is important to again emphasize that an experiment produces an objective way of judging an idea or hypothesis.*

Instructional Activities. The task here is to demonstrate to the students how an experiment tests an idea. The Galileo example is probably the easiest and most fun to examine in detail. Although some historians have asserted that this story of Galileo dropping balls off the tower is not correct, it provides a clear illustration of testing an idea and an opportunity to do a variety of creative things with the class. One instructor actually talked his principal into climbing up on the building's roof to drop objects of different weights and sizes. (In case you want to try this as well, the rationale was as follows: Obviously the instructor had to supervise the exercise, so he couldn't get up there, and clearly neither the school board nor the insurance company would want to have students wandering around the roof. Thus the only person left to help out in this educationally valuable enterprise was the principal. It worked once, but I don't guarantee it.) You need not rise to such heights to produce some stimulating experiments, however.

Start the discussion with the common observation that heavier objects do seem to fall faster than light ones, but is the difference in weight responsible for this difference? What other factors might be involved here? Shape, density, wind resistance all play a role. How can you demonstrate that weight per se is not the main factor? Hold weight constant and manipulate shape. For example, you could take two pieces of paper of equal weight (You might want to go through the ritual of actually weighing them with a balance scale). Next, simply crumple one of them up. Now all you have to do is drop them simultaneously from a height of about 8 feet, and the crumpled one will clearly fall faster than the regular sheet (i.e., hit first). (Instead of the balance scale, you could doublecheck by flattening the formerly crumpled and crumpling the formerly flat piece of paper and trying again.)

Now ask the class if a lighter object could fall faster than a heavier one? You might be able to win a couple of bets on this one, if you present it the right way. Take two balloons of the same size shape and weight; again you may want to actually weigh them. If there is a difference in weight, choose the heavier of the two to be the one that will fall the most slowly. Next, blow up one of them. Which balloon is now the heaviest? The one with the additional weight of the air. It may be less dense, but nonetheless, it is heavier. When they are dropped, the lighter (flat one) balloon will fall more quickly than the heavy balloon, and you win your bets.

Most of the students will never have thought about weight, shape, and density in this way, so there should be some good discussion (arguments) about what it all means. Finally, what did happen is discussed and how the result affects the original idea (the weights fall at the same speed, proving that the idea is wrong).

The analysis of the Pasteur and psychological experiments is a little more complex. Pasteur's experiment involved some assumptions based on his experience that might not be readily apparent. The presence of bacteria was assumed because of the way the wine looked and because of Pasteur's other experiments with bacteria. The point here is that *the results of other experiments can be used to analyze or help analyze a new problem and design a new experiment.* Similarly, the test of the idea is more complex and a little less direct than the Galileo experiment. Pasteur knew from previous work that high temperatures kill bacteria. So the hypothesis of the experiment can be stated as follows: Cloudy particles and bad taste indicate the presence of bacteria. Bacteria may be what is causing the wine to spoil. Bacteria dies at high temperature. If the wine is boiled, the bacteria will die. If the bacteria die, the wine will not spoil. These ideas can be developed in the manner illustrated in the analysis of the Galileo experiment, but the instructor will have to make sure the less obvious aspects of the experiment come out in the discussion.

The psychological experiment is even more complex, and the detailed assumption involved in it are not discussed in this unit. The main point to make is that experiments can be done in ways that will allow us to test ideas about human behavior.

Added bits of information
• Both Newton's and Einstein's analysis of gravity and the attraction of bodies indicate that weight does influence the rate at which a body will fall toward earth. This influence, however, is so small on the earth's surface that it can be ignored.
• Galileo also built a telescope that could be used to view the craters on the moon's surface. His critics refused to believe him or even look through his telescope because Aristotle said that heavenly bodies were perfect; therefore there could not be any holes on the moon.

Unit 4. A Psychological Experiment in Social Interaction

Objective: Conduct and analyze a psychological experiment.

CONDUCTING THE EXPERIMENT

Actually practicing a science is the best way to learn it. Modern psychology, like other branches of science, relies on the experiment as the basis for evaluating hypothesis and explanations. The simple experiment outlined in this unit was selected because it involves an important psychological variable—attention—and it also *usually* works.

Instructional Activities. The directions for conducting the experiment are pretty clear, but there is the tricky problem of keeping the subject from learning how he/she is supposed to act. This can be accomplished by having the students leave their books with you after completing Unit 3 and then assigning groups and selecting which role each person will play in the experiment before beginning to read the unit.

The only problem that we have had with students conducting this experiment is that the subject sometimes runs out of things to say. We have dealt with this problem in three ways. First, select your most talkative students to be subjects. Second, the time blocks can be changed from 5 minutes for each condition to 3 minutes. Finally, we have changed the target words from plural nouns to personal pronouns (I; me; we; us). This change has worked very well. You might even have one group run the study using plural nouns and one using personal pronouns.

ANALYZING THE RESULTS

The experiment has as its idea or hypothesis that if a class of words is followed by attention, those words will increase in frequency. Attention is being manipulated by the experimenter as a way of testing this idea.

Instructional Activities. The students are asked to write out their ideas about why they observed their particular results. Because the analysis of the results involves concepts that are not presented until Unit 6, we postpone the interpretation of the results until then. When you ask the students to write out their ideas, simply be positive and encourage them to discuss what happened in the experiment by looking closely at their data.

Unit 5. Understanding Causes: The Relevance of the Experimental Method to Everyday Life

Objective: Convince the students that science and the experimental method in particular are essential for understanding our daily lives.

The crucial point is that questions about the how and why of everyday events are really questions about causes or functional relations. Further, when we are told that something happened for a particular reason, we should critically analyze that statement to see if it is logical in the same way that we would a statement about cause in a scientific paper.

Instructional Activities. This is a relatively complex unit, and we don't expect the students to completely understand all of the points after one session. We do, however, expect them to get the basic ideas, and we hope that you will periodically point out how we are trying to discover causes when we are analyzing our own behavior in later units.

We begin the discussion of causes in a humorous fashion with the accompanying cartoon. This specific cartoon is not reprinted in the students' workbook, so you may choose to make copies for the students or to use a transparency of it. In the cartoon, the mother takes a very hot pitcher from the dishwasher and places frozen juice concentrate in it. As could be predicted the bottom of the pitcher falls out. The mother then asks her son and daughter what outstanding fact of science has just been proven? The son's reply, (that it was a pretty dumb thing to do!) was not exactly the answer she had anticipated. After everyone has had a good laugh, you should proceed to analyze the cartoon. (The good laugh is very important here because it demonstrates that you can laugh at adult behavior and, by implication, yourself. If you don't find this cartoon

funny, you should reconsider whether you want to teach this class or work with adolescents. Because if you can't laugh at yourself, you could have real trouble dealing with kids.)

In the analysis of the cartoon, the first point to make is that you do not actually prove scientific facts. What is proven or disproven is a principle or theory (i.e., an explanation). In this particular case, the principles involved at the molecular level are really fairly complex, but they can be summarized as the following. When a glass object is heated, it causes an increase in molecular activity. Rapid cooling produces an immediate decrease. At the boundary between the heating and cooling, stress and fracturing are produced; whether the glass breaks is determined by the parameters of the situation. That is, what type of glass is being used, how hot it becomes, how cold, how rapidly it is chilled, and how much of it is exposed to the cold.

Obviously, if you went ahead and told the students this, they would find the whole thing pretty boring and won't learn anything from the discussion. So ask the students what principles they think are involved here. The first task will be to get them to describe what actually happened and to relate the events to one another. The resulting description could be called a procedural explanation, and it could be used to reproduce the phenomenon. Accurate observation and description are important first steps in any science, and you should remind the students of the discussion in Unit 1. After the analysis of what happened, the molecular basis of the process could be presented, but it is not crucial.

Next, ask where most of the explanations we use in everyday life come from. Most of the assertions we make about why things happen to us are so commonplace that it is difficult for us to think of them as explanations. So if the students don't come up with anything right away, then you should have some examples ready to prompt the discussion. Current events can provide a wide range of potential examples, such as the explanations given for why the United States Armed Forces attacked Libya in 1986. Similarly, common sense maxims are another source of everyday explanations to be examined.

A historical example of an explanation that used both governmental authority and common sense was Adolph Hitler's assertion that Germany's financial problems were caused by a conspiracy of Jewish bankers. The logic ran something like this: Germany is a good country; yet Germany has severe financial problems. What is the cause of these problems? Banks, especially international banks, are involved in financial affairs. It follows that the banks must be causing Germany's problems for their own gain. Who are the most prominent bankers? Jews. Therefore, it is a Jewish conspiracy that is causing Germany these problems, so the Jews must be crushed.

Once the class starts discussing possible explanations, it should be easy to move into the analysis of the nature of these explanations as presented in Unit 5. What we hope the students will learn is that most everyday explanations of why things happen are not very good. It won't be too difficult to convince teenagers that most reasons given by adults for why things happen are wrong. The tricky part, of course, is to encourage them to systematically develop better ones.

Unit 6. Operant Behavior and Consequences

Objective: Introduce the concepts of operant behavior and consequences.

OPERANT BEHAVIOR

Operant behavior is the type of response that is affected by its consequences.

CONSEQUENCES

Consequences are events that *follow* the occurrence of an operant response and affect its future probability of occurrence.

It is clear that psychology is not simply concerned with operant behavior; there are many phenomena that a psychologist could study. This program, however, is concerned with operant behavior because it is the most common form of socially significant behavior.

Instructional Activities. The difference between operant (voluntary) behavior and respondent (involuntary) behavior can be illustrated with a certain amount of guile. As you start the discussion, ask a student to write an example of an operant on the board. While the other students are attending to the first, quickly slam a heavy book down on your desk or table (make sure your thumbs or fingers are not under the book). This should produce a loud noise and a startle response from the students. This startle response is a respondent or involuntary reaction. If you get a good, loud, unexpected noise there should be a slight jump, a turn in the direction of the noise, an intake of breath and an increase in heart rate. You can discuss how these reactions are similar to the pupillary reflex. The students should be able to see how the respondents are produced by stimuli that precede (or come before) them. We have since discovered a safer method, which is to use an official's whistle and blow it very hard while the students' attention is misdirected, as before.

Examples of operant responses that can be discussed are Cathy's crawling behavior and the subject's use of plural nouns in the Unit 4 experiment. Cathy's crawling increased or decreased as a function of whether the teachers attended to her crawling. Teacher attention is a stimulus that *followed* her behavior and affected how often she crawled. Therefore, attention would be called a consequence. The same analysis can be done for the experiment in Unit 4.

The notion of consequences can be demonstrated by playing the old game of hotter–colder. That is, a student leaves the room and some object is hidden. The student then returns and tries to find the object by responding to the consequence hotter–colder when he/she moves in one direction or another. The feedback (you're getting hotter/colder) influences how we move next.

Finally, to complete the unit, look at the Garfield cartoon. It is both an example of consequences (the chair dropping on his head when he scratches John's leg) and a theme of the program that will be developed later—trying to anticipate possible future consequences of actions.

Unit 7. Reinforcement: Positive and Negative

Objective: Teach the scientific definitions of positive and negative reinforcement, and provide enough relevant examples so that the students learn how these processes influence behavior.

Please note. This unit is quite long and contains several of the most important concepts in the book: You should take your time and discuss the ideas enough to ensure that the students clearly understand them. As a consequence, the unit may require two or even three class sessions to complete. There is also a table of definitions and behavioral effects that summarizes the concepts taught in this and the next two units. Tell the students to use the table as a prompt or reminder to help them in their work.

POSITIVE REINFORCEMENT

Positive reinforcement is the most important behavioral process presented in the book. Positive reinforcement plays a major role in influencing how we behave in most everyday situations. Positive reinforcement is
the process of increasing the frequency of a response by delivering a
positive reinforcer contingent on the occurrence of the response. In this
definition, there are two important subcomponents that need to be
discussed: *positive reinforcer* and *contingent*.

Instructional Activities. Instruction focuses on identifying (1) positive
reinforcers and (2) how to deliver them. In all of the examples of positive
reinforcement, these features are present: A *consequence* is *delivered
immediately contingent* on the occurrence of a response, and that response *increases* in frequency. For it to be most effective in changing
behavior, the positive reinforcer should be delivered immediately after
the response occurs. The relation between the occurrence of the response
and the delivery of the reinforcer is called the "contingency." If a positive
reinforcer is available any time, delivering it after a response will not
increase the probability of the response. For example, if Danny's mom
made dessert every night irrespective of whether his room was clean,
telling him she made dessert that night because he cleaned his room
would have no effect on room-cleaning behavior. As you discuss the
examples, continue to ask the following questions:

1. What was the positive reinforcer?
2. How and when was it delivered?
3. What response was reinforced?
4. Was the reinforcer delivered contingently?

Another point about reinforcers that frequently confuses people is that
the same stimulus is not necessarily a reinforcer for everyone. For example, most people would consider money a positive reinforcer. We work
for it and increase the frequency of responses that produce it. But money
is not a positive reinforcer for everyone; consider, for instance, such
individuals as hermits, nuns who have taken vows of poverty, or, paradoxically, extremely wealthy people. The delivery of money contingent
on the behavior of such persons would *not* increase the frequency of
those responses and thus would not be considered a positive reinforcer.
Reinforcers are defined by their function (or effect) and not what they
look like (or our expectations).

We usually base our expectations about reinforcers on our own likes and dislikes. For example, if I like chocolate milk shakes, I would expect chocolate milk shakes to be a positive reinforcer for another person. I might try to reinforce another person's nice behavior by buying the person a chocolate milk shake when he/she is being nice. But that person may have eaten too much chocolate at one time as a child and now gets violently ill whenever anyone even mentions chocolate. Instead of reinforcing the behavior, my offer of a chocolate milk shake may be a punishing stimulus. Similarly, stimuli are often expected to be punishing, but they may actually function as a reinforcer. For example, if you reprimand a student for a particular response and that response *increases* in frequency, then a reprimand is a positive reinforcer for that student.

The idea that positive reinforcers vary from person to person can be illustrated by the following exercise.

Have each student independently write a list of at least 10 things that would be a positive reinforcer for her/him. The events could be activities such as playing basketball, going to a movie, eating a cookie, being given a dollar for receiving an A on a paper, etc. Next, put a column on the board, numbered 1 through 10, for each student in the class.

George	Sally	Jim
1.	1.	1.
2.	2.	2.
3.	3.	3.
4.	4.	4.
5.	5.	5.
6.	6.	6.
7.	7.	7.
8.	8.	8.
9.	9.	9.
10.	10.	10.

Then pick out some behavior, such as studying or making the bed. Then ask the students to take turns reading their lists. The question is, "if someone gave (granted) you ——— (an item from a student's list) after you studied, would you study more?" Each student answers "yes" or "no." "Yes" indicates the stimulus is probably a reinforcer for that person. "No" means it probably isn't.

After going through the list, you should have a patterns of yes and no on the blackboard.

George
1. Yes, Yes, Yes
2. Yes, Yes, Yes
3. No, No, Yes
4. No, Yes, Yes
10. No, No, No

By looking at these results, the students will be able to see that the things they select as reinforcers may or may not be reinforcers for other people. A faster way of making this point is to ask each student to raise his/her hand if he/she would pay extra to have onion on a hamburger. This should start the discussion of how something might be a positive reinforcer for one person and not another.

Another exercise that can be used in this lesson is based on one of the most pervasive stories in the mythology of operant psychology, "the famous professor whose students reinforced him for lecturing with one hand on the blackboard." According to the story, he soon spent all of his time in class with one hand on the blackboard. There are many variations on this story, but you can use the basic element to demonstrate how positive reinforcement can affect behavior. Have one of the students leave the room before beginning the class session. While this student is out of the room, select some behavior of his/hers that the class will reinforce. The response selected should be easy to pick out—that is, a very simple behavioral definition that all the students can agree on. Raising the hand before speaking and praising or speaking positively about another person are two possible responses. As the positive reinforcer, you and the other students should smile and be attentive immediately after the response. This procedure should be continued for about 15 minutes to half an hour. Then stop and discuss what effect the positive reinforcer had on the frequency of the response. An important consideration in selecting a student for the demonstration is the assumption that attention of this sort will be a reinforcer for the person. This will not always be the case, so select someone you are pretty sure will be responsive to attention. Another consideration is picking a response that occurs at a relatively frequent rate that is, not a verbal response of a student who never speaks in class. Over the course of the period, there should have been a noticeable increase in the frequency of the response. This exercise is an informal variation of the Greenspoon (1955) experiment and the study of Cathy's crawling behavior. After discussing the demonstration, have the students review the results and interpretation of their Greenspoon experiments.

NEGATIVE REINFORCEMENT

Negative reinforcement is a very tricky but important concept. It is also a difficult procedure to demonstrate because it involves aversive, often painful, stimuli. Negative reinforcement plays an important role in human behavior, however, because we often do things *not* to produce positive reinforcers but *to escape or avoid* negative reinforcers. Negative reinforcement is the process of increasing the frequency of a response by removing a negative reinforcer contingent on the occurrence of a response. This definition is the same as that of positive reinforcement except that the stimulus is a negative reinforcer and, most important, it is removed or subtracted rather than added.

Instructional Activities. Instruction on negative reinforcement focuses on identifying negative reinforcers and how their removal influences behavior. A very simple example of negative reinforcement would be the response of taking aspirin or some other pain reliever when you have a headache. The response of taking the medicine is negatively reinforced by the removal of pain. The negative reinforcer is the pain of the headache. After discussing a few such simple examples of negative reinforcement, you can try the negative reinforcement demonstration.

A very short demonstration of negative reinforcement can be conducted by using a mildly aversive stimulus such as a high squeaking noise. You can use a small portable cassette recorder to produce your noise source. Obnoxious noises can be found all around you—for example, a badly muffled motorcycle or snowmobile engine, a beginning student practicing the violin, the thunking hissing noise when the phonograph needle is stuck at the end of a record, and so on. Record about 15 minutes of such a stimulus. You can now use this stimulus as a negative reinforcer by turning it off for a period of time contingent on the occurrence of a response.

The steps in actually conducting the demonstration are very simple. Select a student to be the subject, and then explain to him/her that the noise will be turned off for 10 seconds contingent on some response. *Do not* tell the student the specific response you have selected. Simply turn the tape on and wait until the response occurs. Always pick out a response that is easy to observe. In this case, moving either hand to an ear or just moving one hand or the other, would make a good target response (it is very likely that the student will do something with his/her hands in this situation). When the student's hand moves, turn off the tape.

If the student's hand stops moving, wait 10 seconds and turn the tape back on; again turn it off when the student's hand moves. It is difficult to diagram a negative reinforcement escape and avoidance contingency but it looks something like this:

S_1(Noise on)   R--------S_2(Noise off for 10 seconds)

As long as the response continues to occur within the 10-second S_2 period, the noise continues to be off. If it does not occur for 10 seconds, S_1 (Noise on) is presented. Another response will again remove S_1 for 10 seconds.

Over the course of about 10 to 15 minutes of the escape–avoidance contingency (only run the procedure long enough to consistently produce the escape–avoidance), an interesting thing should happen to the responding. In the beginning, the student may make a response that turns off the noise but may stop the response until the noise comes back on again. But soon, the time between responses may become short enough to avoid some of the scheduled noise. This process may continue until the student is moving a hand at fairly high frequency and avoiding all of the noise. This, of course, is the reasonable and expected outcome of the procedure, but think how odd it looks. If someone were to come into the room after the avoidance had developed, the student would be moving a hand in a strange (to the observer) manner for apparently no reason.

After completing and discussing the demonstration exercise, a more important point should be made about negative reinforcement. In social interactions, the person who is negatively reinforced may accidently positively reinforce another person for being obnoxious. In the example of Sara and her sister, the sister is being a pest. Sara finally said yes to escape her nagging, but saying yes is also a positive reinforcer for the sister's nagging behavior. As a consequence, we would expect the sister to pester Sara more in the future. Such behavior can obviously cause arguments and a lot of tension between the two sisters, so in the long run they both might lose by this type of interaction. To finish the lesson, you should carefully review the study guide questions.

Unit 8. Punishment and Response Cost

Objective: Teach the students the scientific procedures of punishment and response cost and the social limitations of their use.

PUNISHMENT AND RESPONSE COST

These are procedures that reduce or decrease the frequency of the response that produces them. Individuals, and society in general, often attempt to use some form of punishment procedure to eliminate an undesirable response. These efforts are frequently unsuccessful because the procedures are either scientifically wrong or inappropriately applied. The two procedures are complementary to the two reinforcement procedures. *Punishment* is the delivery of a stimulus *contingent* on the occurrence of a response that *decreases* the future probability of occurrence of that response. This is essentially the same procedure as a positive reinforcement, but instead of a positive reinforcer being added, *a punishing stimulus* (*negative reinforcer*) is delivered. Similarly *response cost* is the *subtraction* of a stimulus *contingent* on the occurrence of a response that *decreases* the future probability of occurrence of that response. Again, the procedure is the same as a negative reinforcement, but the stimulus removed is a *positive reinforcer* rather than a negative reinforcer.

Instructional Activities. The main focus of instruction in this unit is on the limitation of punishment and response cost procedures. It is important that students understand that even when the procedure has the desired effect, there are often undesirable side effects. These side effects have to do with the reaction of the person who is being punished. Frankly, the major reason for including this unit in the program is that people often try to use punishment and then cannot understand why the other person becomes upset. Punishment and response cost are procedures that should *not* be used in everyday life. These procedures should *only* be used by professionals.

After discussing the examples of punishment and response cost as used by professionals, ask the students how they would feel if a friend tried to punish them. A person can react to a punishment or response cost procedure in one or more of three ways. First, if there are constraints on the individual's freedom, the response in question will decrease in frequency. Second, and more likely, the person will simply leave the situation and avoid the individual doing the punishing. Finally, the person may reciprocate in kind; that is, try to do the same thing to the other individual (or to another, less powerful, individual). Even in the first instance, in which punishment has been apparently effective, the person may develop an aversion or dislike for the punisher, which can interfere with future interactions. Consider, for example, our reaction to the presence of a police officer. Even though we may not be doing anything wrong, there is a general tendency (unless you personally know the officer) to leave the area. This is because the police are associated with punishment.

Obviously, this is essentially a discussion unit. There are no exercises to demonstrate either procedure. The hope is that students will learn about these procedures and why they should not be used in interpersonal interactions.

Unit 9. Extinction and Time-Out from Positive Reinforcement

Objective: Teach the students the concept of extinction and how to use the procedure of extinction. In addition, teach the students the procedure of time-out from positive reinforcement.

EXTINCTION

This is the recommended procedure for reducing the frequency of a particular response. Extinction involves identifying the reinforcement contingency that is maintaining the frequency of a particular response and eliminating it. If the stimulus that was reinforcing the behavior is no longer delivered contingent on the occurrence of that response, the response will decrease in frequency. The effect of extinction is less dramatic than that of a punishment or of response cost procedures, but when it is combined with the reinforcement of incompatible responses, there are no negative side effects.

Whether we wish to acknowledge it or not, we all try to influence other people's behavior. We try a variety of techniques, from cajoling to coercion, but the most effective form of persuasion psychologists have discovered is the use of extinction for the undesirable response and positive reinforcement for a desirable response(s). Almost all of the procedures discussed and recommended to students in the remainder of the program involve these two procedures. As a consequence, it is very important that the students learn to analyze what may be reinforcing an undesirable response and how to use extinction to eliminate it.

Instructional Activities. Because the next unit consists of an experiment using extinction and reinforcement of incompatible responses, instructional activities for this unit involve both mastering the ideas and preparing to conduct the experiment. After discussing the study guide, the class should review the Greenspoon experiment. Remember that in the experimental condition, plural nouns were followed by a social positive reinforcer (attention in the form of expressions of interest); next, the experimenter stopped paying attention to the plural nouns. The frequency of plural nouns increased when they were reinforced and decreased when the experimenter stopped reinforcing them. Extinction involves stopping the delivery of a consequence and the observation of a decrease in the frequency of the behavior. The procedure used in the Greenspoon experiment—not attending, or ignoring—is the most common form of extinction procedure. It assumes that the behavior was strengthened and is now maintained by the attention it produces. If you ignore the behavior, it will decrease in strength (go away).

The example of parents putting their child to bed is one that has produced some very interesting discussion. Usually, several of the students will take the child's side and argue that the parents should not ignore him. They will insist that the child should be allowed to stay up or that the parents should reason with him and come up with a mutually agreed upon bedtime. This position of course ignores the perspective of the parent and the fact that the child has already refused to compromise. Rather than changing the example, we have used it as a stimulus for a brief discussion about seeing the other person's side of a dispute. Also, when reasoning fails, it is better to use extinction for a brief period of time than to fight over the same thing time and time again. You will not convince all the students, but the discussion will be stimulating.

Optional demonstration of extinction. A very convincing demonstration of extinction can be conducted, but it takes great concentration, calmness, and a real sense of humor. As a consequence, you may not wish to use it, or perhaps you should practice it in advance of trying it with the class. The demonstration is based on the premise that every student, given the opportunity, would enjoy getting the teacher's goat; the exercise simply sanctions this effort. The class is told that they can pick two people whose job it will be to make you mad. The rules are that they can not touch you, make physical gestures, or use profanity of any type. A violation of a rule stops the game. The students can, however, comment on your intelligence or your appearance. Two further constraints or rules are that both the students and yourself must stay seated throughout, and you should be separated by 5 to 10 feet. When you explain the exercise, the students should be very enthusiastic; if they are not, cancel it. They will know you are up to something, but they will try anyway. This means that you need to be able to ignore and not respond to taunts they can come up with. If you do respond, it blows the demonstration, and it could cause difficulties in your subsequent interactions with the class. The best way to ignore the remarks is to adopt a slight smile, relax, and concentrate on your breathing. If you cannot ignore a student who is calling you a "stupid turkey," then do not try this exercise. The students will begin with great energy, continue for about 5 minutes, and then slow down considerably so that after 10 minutes they will have stopped or are obviously about to. Unkind remarks are frequently made because of reactions on the part of the other person. If the other person does not react, the behavior will decrease. This exercise will demonstrate this relationship; the same points can be made by discussion or role playing however.

INCOMPATIBLE RESPONSES

When two responses are incompatible, it is physically impossible to make both responses at the same time. The idea of incompatible responses is important because the extinction of an undesirable response can be accelerated if we reinforce another response at the same time.

Instructional Activities. The idea of incompatible responses is quite simple and can be easily demonstrated. It was rumored that former President Gerald Ford could not walk and chew gum at the same time. Actually, Gerald Ford was one of our more athletically accomplished presidents; nonetheless, the story illustrates the idea. Smiling and frowning are incompatible. Talking and eating crackers are incompatible. Walking and looking behind you, while not totally incompatible, are difficult to do at the same time. Have the students think of a number of pairs of incompatible responses, and then the students should try to do some of the responses at the same time.

TIME-OUT FROM POSITIVE REINFORCEMENT

In time-out from positive reinforcement, the individual who has been earning positive reinforcers for engaging in a particular behavior is not allowed to do so for a period of time. The opportunity to earn positive reinforcers is removed, contingent on the occurrence of an undesirable response. This procedure is very effective if in fact the individual is earning positive reinforcers at a reasonable rate. On the other hand, research with animals demonstrates that the animal will actually work to get into time-out if it has been on either an extinction schedule or long schedule of reinforcement. This is one of the reasons why many of the so-called time-out procedures used in schools and institutions do not work.

Instructional Activities. Time-out is not a major concept for self-management, so the instruction will consist of simply discussing the examples in the book. The major points to be made are the differences between time-out and extinction and the fact that reinforcement must be available to the person for time-out to work.

Unit 10. A Demonstration Experiment Using Extinction and the Reinforcement of Incompatible Responses

Objective: Conduct and analyze an experiment using extinction and the reinforcement of incompatible responses.

Extinction and positive reinforcement of incompatible responses are two of the most useful procedures that anyone can learn. The experiment is designed to give the students actual practice using them and analyzing their effects.

Instructional Activities. First, go through each step of the experiment in class to ensure that each student understands the procedure. Informed consent is an important concept so not only discuss it, but also have the students role-play asking another student to participate in the experiment. You might also ask the students to pair up and have them decide in class who is going to be the main experimenter and who is going to be responsible for recording the data.

Because the experiment will be conducted over several days, you will need to ask students to bring their data with them to class sessions. You can then spend about 10 minutes at the beginning of those sessions to review the data and to check whether there have been any difficulties. Finally, when the students have collected all of their data, you should schedule a whole class session for them to analyze their results and write their reports. The reports will not be very sophisticated, but be sure that the data are correctly graphed and that the students have a good idea whether or not the procedure worked.

Unit 11. Shaping

Objective: Teach students the procedure of shaping and how it can be used to teach new behaviors.

SHAPING

Shaping consists of the systematic use of three behavioral procedures: positive reinforcement, extinction, and successive approximations of the target behavior. Shaping is an important process because it produces new behaviors. Although most of the cases described in the unit involve the systematic use of shaping, the process does occur naturally.

Instructional Activities. After reviewing the study guide, begin the general discussion by looking at the cartoon. The cartoon illustrates two major points of shaping. Hitting the target's bulls' eye from a distance with the arrow is the target behavior (there must be a pun in there somewhere), and the beginning point of shaping is to reinforce a response the person can already make. Reinforcing this response results in an increase in its frequency and that of similar responses. One of these responses will be closer to the target behavior. This response is then reinforced, and the old response (the one that was originally reinforced) is now extinguished. This procedure is repeated until finally the target behavior is produced.

These points can be made again by reviewing the examples in the unit. Then you should call on individual students to answer the questions on page 64 in the students' workbook. Finally, as a group, you should select a new target behavior and decide how it could be shaped.

Teaching a 6-year-old child who is physically capable of walking but only crawls to walk would be a good behavior to analyze in terms of designing a shaping program. But use your imagination here; there is no single right answer.

Added bit of information
• The technical name of shaping is the "differential reinforcement of successive approximations." This, of course, is a mouthful and it is not surprising that the procedure is called shaping.

Unit 12. Stimulus Control: Discrimination

Objective: Teach the students how discriminative stimuli influence behavior and how discriminative stimuli are produced.

DISCRIMINATIVE STIMULUS

A discriminative stimulus is one that precedes the response and increases the probability that the response will occur. A discriminative stimulus influences behavior because it is associated with the reinforcement of that response, whereas other stimuli are associated with the nonreinforcement of that response. Again, positive reinforcement and extinction are involved in what is called discrimination training. Discriminative stimuli are very important in social behavior. The cues we give one another indicate which responses are appropriate and will be reinforced. Consider how difficult it would be if you had no idea what would happen after you made a response.

Instructional Activities. A place to begin the lesson is the example of Tommy asking his mother for a cookie. Here, one stimulus (a smiling mother) is associated with the reinforcement of the response of asking for a cookie, whereas another stimulus (frowning mother) is associated with extinction. This makes it possible to see how reinforcement and extinction are involved in discrimination training. You can also discuss how the success of more appropriate requests, such as asking to go to a movie or stay overnight, may be related to discriminative stimuli.

Next, you can demonstrate discrimination training by running a variation on the old game "Simon Says." If you remember the game, the stimulus "Simon Says," meant you could make the response and be reinforced, but if you made the response when the stimulus was absent, you had to start over. You can have a contest among the students by asking a variety of simple questions about psychology. The student receives a point for each answer if you gave the discriminative stimulus and none if you did not. Use a verbal phrase as the S^D before asking a question and call on the first person who raises a hand. If the S^D is not given and no one raises a hand, just go on to the next question. You can use the game as both a demonstration of discrimination training and a fun review of earlier units. After the game, point out how your verbal discriminative stimulus influenced the students' behavior.

The importance of discriminative stimuli for social behavior can be discussed in conjunction with the example on page 68 in the students' workbook. Finally, the fact that a person can become discriminative for negative reinforcement can be illustrated by analyzing the Garfield cartoon on page 71 in the workbook.

Unit 13. Stimulus Control: Generalization

Objective: Demonstrate how our previous experience with discriminative stimuli helps us to respond to new situations.

GENERALIZATION

Generalization is the process of emitting an old response (one we already know) in the presence of a novel stimulus. Generalization is based on discrimination. If we encounter a new stimulus or situation, and we recognize it (discriminate) as being similar to one in which a particular response has been reinforced in the past, that response is how we will act in the new situation. If the situation is very different, we will not know how to act. Obviously, both discrimination and generalization are very important in learning concepts or rules. For example, the experiment in discrimination training, in Unit 14, actually produces a generalized rule—select male names (primarily; secondarily, select *b*).

Instructional Activities. Because generalization is based on discrimination, begin the discussion by reviewing discrimination training, and then move to the example of naming dogs and cats. This is a clear example of conceptual or rule behavior. Distinguishing between dogs and cats and generalizing to new examples of dogs may not be as formal or as sophisticated to some of us as Einstein's conceptualizations in the theory of relativity, but it is conceptual behavior nonetheless.

Probably more important for the student are the examples of how generalization can influence social behavior—that is, how we respond to new situations or new people. The example on page 73 in the students' workbook is especially relevant. The judgment of how someone will act, based on appearance, is a generalization error, because there is no consistent relation between appearance and behavior. Biased people try to assert that there is a relation—for example, black people are X; fat people are Y—but psychologists have yet to discover any such clear relationship. Just as correct generalization is very important, we must learn how to avoid generalization errors.

A good demonstration of generalization as indicated earlier in the unit is the discrimination training experiment. If your students are similar to mine, because Unit 14 has not been assigned no one will have read it. You can therefore use it to demonstrate how successive discriminations will produce a generalized rule.

Unit 14. An Experiment in Discrimination Training

Objective: Conduct and analyze an experiment in discrimination training.

DISCRIMINATION TRAINING

The experiment consists of a sequence of stimuli designed to produce the concept "male"; names are the S^D. The sequence begins with the single discrimination between the letter *b* as the S^D and all other letters until the name of the male animal is produced. Then male surnames are produced with *b*'s in them. Finally, in the transition stimulus pair 11, boy–girl, to pair 12, Roy–Gayle, the *b* is eliminated and the concept of male names as the essential feature of the S^D should be established.

Instructional Activities. Because you have taken the students through the experiment in Unit 13, they should have a good idea of how the procedures go. You should review the procedures with the students, having them take turns being the experimenter. Next, have them prepare the answer sheets that they will give their subjects. Ask them to conduct the experiment before the next class session. In the next session, you can work through the data with the students, assisting them when necessary; but try to get them to do as much of the graphing and interpretation as they can on their own. After everyone has prepared his/her own report, you can discuss the results, having the students compare their data and interpretations with one another. Finally, you need to make sure that the students understand how discrimination and generalization are involved in the experiment.

Unit 15. Observational Learning: Modeling, Imitation, and Identification

Objective: Provide the students with information about how celebrities, idols, role models, and the like, can indirectly influence their own behavior. The task here is to make students aware of some subtle factors that affect their judgments of goals and aspirations.

OBSERVATIONAL LEARNING

This is a general label for the set of processes discussed in this unit, in which observing a model engage in some response for which she/he is positively reinforced affects the probability that the observer will make the same or similar response in the near future.

Instructional Activities. One way of illustrating how observing prominent people can influence our behavior is to have the students list the five females and five males they most admire or would want to be like. Then have the students list their favorite activities, clothes, records, books, TV shows, movies, and other things about themselves, such as hair style and general fashion. Finally, ask the students to compare their lists of favorite things with the characteristics of the people they admire. There will probably be considerable overlap between how their idols dress, talk, and so on, and their own behavior. This activity should provide a foundation for discussing why they think this happens and how the material presented in the unit helps to explain the phenomenon.

A second useful exercise is to analyze a number of magazine advertisements in terms of how the advertisers are attempting to influence the public's behavior. You should have no difficulty collecting examples of cigarette, alcohol, and/or automobile ads that show the featured person gaining love, recognition, prestige, and so forth, because the individual is using the product. Ask the students to describe television advertisements that try to do the same thing. An active discussion of how the processes of observational learning can be used to manipulate a person's responses without the person being aware of it should follow.

Although observational learning procedures can be used in a manipulative fashion, it is important to end the discussion with the point that observational learning can be a very valuable and positive way of acquiring new skills and goals. Again, the main objective is to make the students aware that these processes affect them every day and to teach them how they work.

Unit 16. Starting a Fad—"Do Elephants Really Pole-Vault?": A Demonstration of the Power of Observational Learning

Objective: This demonstration exercise is designed to be fun, and the major objective of the unit is simply that.

The exercise is clearly an optional component of the program. The factors determining whether you try it with your class/group are time and the number of adolescents in the program. Although the exercise is conducted outside the meeting time, it still takes considerable in-class effort and should not be attempted unless you have 10 weeks or more for the program. Similarly, the study requires more people than the other projects. A minimum of 10 students is needed to carry out these procedures. They need not be in a single section or group, but they must be able to cooperate.

Instructional Activities. Your task in this project is to act as a consultant to the students. All the information they need to conduct the procedures is provided in the unit. They will, however, need some assistance in getting organized and deciding assignments. It probably will take one class session to get the project started and 10–15 minutes in subsequent meetings to review progress and decide what should be done next. Remember that this project is basically for the fun of it, so keep track of what the students are doing, but don't worry too much about it.

Unit 17. Classical Conditioning: Fear and Anxiety

Objective: Provide the students with a basic understanding of emotional responding and how what we call emotions can influence our overall behavior. In addition, it is important that the students learn how emotional responses are caused and what a person can do to eliminate or control them.

FEAR

Fear is an intense emotional response originally produced when the autonomic nervous system (ANS) is aroused by such stimuli as pain or sudden loud noises. Although there are many important situations in which fear is appropriate, fear can become a very debilitating reaction because it conditions so easily. In the conditioning process, other stimuli associated with the unconditioned stimulus come to have the power to elicit the fear response. Those stimuli can then become associated with other stimulus events, which in turn come to elicit a fear response. In this manner, stimuli that should not naturally provoke fear do, in fact, cause the person to become fearful.

ANXIETY

Although there is a lot we don't know about anxiety, in most cases what people are talking about when they say they are anxious appears to be a low-intensity conditioned fear response.

Instructional Activities. The key concept in this unit is the respondent. The students must understand what a respondent looks like and how it works before they can understand emotional responding. This can be done very effectively by first discussing the example of the pupillary reflex and then demonstrating how it works. You will need a small penlight. If you don't have one, you can probably borrow one from a physician. For the demonstration, you will need two volunteers—one to be the subject and the second to be an observer. Also, the light in the room must be dim for the demonstration to work. Have the subject sit in a chair in a relaxed posture with the head slightly back. Now he/she should close one eye and hold the lids of the other open with the thumb and forefinger. The observer should be placed in a position from which the subject's pupil can be easily seen. Next, shine the penlight into the subject's pupil and ask the observer to describe what is happening. The observer should report seeing the subject's pupil become smaller (constrict). After the observer has reported, you can ask the subject if she/he did anything to make the pupil constrict. The answer should be no, because the process occurs automatically. You may wish to repeat the demonstration with other members of the class.

A related demonstration that is easier to do but harder for the observer to see the effects, consists of dark-adapting a person and then observing the pupils constrict when the lighting is increased. Simply send two volunteers into a dark closet for about 5 minutes (first make sure that they are not afraid of the dark). Five minutes should be enough time for dark adaptation to occur; that is, their pupils will become maximally dilated. When they come out, have them hold their eye lids open with thumb and forefinger, and the observers should again see the pupils quickly constrict. A point here is that without specialized equipment, it is almost impossible to observe the pupils dilate, but it should be obvious that the process occurs because the subjects' pupils will be very large when they come out of the dark room.

In discussing the respondent, it is important to make the students understand that these reactions are automatic. They occur because they are built into us and are elicited when the correct stimulus is presented.

You are now ready to discuss and demonstrate respondent conditioning. First, review the example of Pavlov and his dogs. Does the process occur in humans? Yes, and you can use a similar procedure to demonstrate it. The demonstration is based on the salivary response to a moderate acid solution. The response to too much vinegar in the oil and vinegar dressing or too much lemon in the lemonade is puckering of the mouth followed by a rush of saliva. With a little bit of luck, you should be able to condition this response to a tone. You will need the following equipment for the exercise: a squirt bottle such as those used by athletes to get a drink, a length of small tubing, a strong lemon juice mixture, and something to produce a tone (tuning fork, pitch pipe, or similar device).

Again you will need two volunteers, one person to assist you and the second to be the subject. Prepare your lemon juice mixture in advance, and test it on yourself. If it makes your mouth pucker and water, it is ok. If on the other hand, it makes you gag, then it is too strong; if no reaction, it is too weak. Adjust the mix until you get the right response, then fill the squirt bottle with that mixture and attach the tube. You want to squirt a small amount of the juice into the subject's mouth—too much and gagging will occur. Also because timing is important, you should probably be the person who controls the delivery of the lemon juice. Your assistant will sound the tone.

Instruct the subject to keep track of how much saliva is being produced. The easiest way is for the person simply to count how many times he/she swallows. If the procedure works, the increased saliva flow will be easily discriminated. Next, have the person sit in a comfortable chair and relax. Place the tube in the person's mouth at the side and to the rear where the taste buds for sour and bitter are located. The assistant should be seated behind the subject.

> Sound tone --------------------- (5 seconds)
>   Inject fluid ---------- Saliva
>
> Wait 1 minute. Then give the subject a drink of water.
> Repeat the procedure 5 times. On the 6th trial, only
> present the tone.

If all goes well, the subject should produce an increased amount of saliva after the tone even though the lemon juice was not used. Remember, the reaction will not be as strong as that to the unconditioned stimulus (UCS), but it will be greater than if nothing had happened or to the tone alone if it had not been paired with the lemon juice.

One more thing you can do with this demonstration is to have the subject try to imagine biting into a juicy lemon and sucking out the juice. If the person has good visual imagery, his/her mouth should start watering. The main point here is that words and other subtle stimuli can come to elicit respondents as well as the more obvious conditioned stimuli.

Although saliva is not what we usually think of when we talk about emotional responses, the process for their conditioning and generalization is the same. Thus the demonstration can be used to analyze the development of a conditioned fear response. For instance, many people are afraid to go to the dentist. Why is that? In my case, it began when I was 12. A large permanent molar simply fell apart and had to be pulled. Unfortunately, my dentist was not very good. He didn't get the nerve deadened, and it also took him several tries to actually get it out. As a consequence, I had an extremely painful, fear-provoking experience that was associated with that dentist, the dentist's office, the smell and sounds of a dentist's office, and so on.

To make a long story short, for many years I was terrified of dentists and ate dozens of aspirin whenever I got a toothache rather than going to the dentist. Eventually, I was driven to seek help because of increasingly painful problems with my teeth. Fortunately, this dentist was extremely good. Nonetheless, I would still have anxiety attacks when entering the office. These continued even though this particular dentist had never been paired with the extreme pain of the first. I was finally able to get rid of the conditioned response by a systematic program of relaxation and controlled breathing, which I would begin before getting out of the car to enter the office. The program worked because the relaxation and even breathing were incompatible with the anxiety responses and the UCS (pain) was no longer paired with the conditioned stimulus (CS).

This anecdote, which is actually true (unfortunately), illustrates some important features of conditioned fear reactions. First, they are not rational. Even when young, I knew I should go to the dentist for a toothache and that postponing it would only make the situation worse. Still my fear of the dentist was so great that I forced myself to endure far more pain from bad teeth than ever would have been produced by going to the dentist. The essential point here is that to avoid the immediate fear-provoking stimulus, people will do things which have much more important long-term negative consequences than the actual feared stimulus.

Second, the fear response is automatic, so the person often feels there is nothing he/she can do about it. This feeling of helplessness can have a general detrimental effect on the person's self-concept and overall behavior.

Finally, conditioned fears can be conquered. It is important to remember that in this section, we are discussing inappropriate conditioned fears that are interfering with the person's normal life. Paradoxically, while such fears are not rational, the first step in dealing with them is a logical analysis of your personal past. The objective of this analysis is to discover the conditioning history (experiences) that may have produced the fear response and to specifically determine what it is in the present situation that is producing the fear response. Then it is possible to design a program such as that used by Gross and Brigham (1980) to eliminate the conditioned response.

We have not talked specifically about anxiety responses in this analysis, but, in general, all of the points made about inappropriate conditioned fear responses apply to anxiety reactions as well. The term *anxiety* as it is commonly used refers to a generalized low-level conditioned fear. The way that a person should go about dealing with specific anxiety reactions is essentially the same as the steps described by Gross and Brigham (1980).

Because there are two additional units on dealing with fear and anxiety, you need not go into greater detail here. If you have students who are concerned about these issues, assign them Units 23 and 25 for the next class. Then it should be possible to systematically work through a simple anxiety problem such as fear of participating in class. If you discover a serious psychological problem, be sure that the student sees the school counselor as the first step in getting professional help.

To reiterate, the main objectives of this unit are to give the students a basic understanding of fear and anxiety and to demonstrate that they can be controlled.

Added bit of information

• It is somewhat ironic that Pavlov is known worldwide as a psychologist because during his life he insisted that he was not a psychologist. Actually, he didn't think very much of the psychology of his time because all introspective psychology seemed to study was mental states. Because Pavlov didn't believe that mental states could be studied scientifically, psychology struck him as a big waste of time. I don't know if he would be happier with this psychology book, but I certainly hope so.

Part II. Applying Behavior Analysis Skills

The units in this section involve applying or using the procedures that have been learned in Part I. The first step in application is analysis, to determine which factors (reinforcers, discriminative stimuli) might be involved in a particular situation, and how they should be changed. Such analysis is also a major focus of instruction in this section. To help the students, a number of examples of self-management projects completed by other students in earlier programs and classes are presented in this section. The projects reported here are all essentially correct. They have been edited somewhat, however, to increase their instructional value. Nonetheless, each accurately presents a set of procedures and results produced by a student participating in a self-management program. They are provided not as data to support the scientific validity of the program; rather, their primary function is to illustrate how self-management procedures can be used systematically to deal with everyday problems.

There are also three applied projects in which the students are asked to actually use the procedures that have been discussed. The first is an effort to improve a friendship by having the student change the way he/she acts with a friend. The recommended procedures are positive reinforcement and extinction. Next, ask the students to negotiate a contract with their parents (or guardians) to solve some simple behavioral conflict. The final project is a self-management effort in which the students are required to select a behavior of their own, analyze the factors influencing how often it occurs, and then develop and implement a program to change it. These projects are the culmination of the instruction, and the student's success on them will greatly influence whether they use the ideas and procedures presented in the manual in their everyday lives. Your role in this section is essentially that of a consultant with whom the students can check their ideas and receive suggestions on how they might deal with a particular problem. Again, the focus of the instructional effort is on having the students produce as much of their own analysis as possible.

Unit 18. A Laboratory Case History

Objective: Teach the students how to use the concepts they have learned in order to analyze how Sarah changed her life.

ANALYSIS, POSITIVE REINFORCEMENT, AND EXTINCTION

Sarah's efforts to change how things were going consisted of analyzing her pattern of interaction with the other students and changing the way she acted. Instead of fighting, arguing, or being mean in return, she learned to positively reinforce other people when they were nice and ignore (extinguish) unkind responses.

Instructional Activities. The main function of this unit is to show the students how someone the same general age dealt with a set of everyday problems by using self-management procedures. The focus of instruction is on identifying how Sarah analyzed situations and what procedures she used to change her own behavior and that of others. You should especially concentrate on analyzing (1) the positive reinforcers she employed and (2) the way that ignoring was used as an extinction procedure.

In addition, you could ask the students if they were ever in similar situations and how they might now handle them.

Unit 19. Applying Behavior Analysis Skills with Others

Objective: Teach the students the concepts of reciprocity and equity and that how a person acts influences how other people respond to him/her.

RECIPROCITY AND EQUITY

These are key concepts for understanding and improving social interactions. Adolescents generally have a limited perspective on how their behavior affects other people.

Instructional Activities. This is essentially a discussion unit to prepare the students to conduct the behavior modification project in the next unit. Nonetheless, it is very important that the students understand these concepts. In addition to discussing the study guide and reviewing the examples in the unit, you should be prepared to pose a variety of questions concerning equity and reciprocity. It is important that the questions be stated both from the perspective of the student and from that of other people. The following example questions cover both perspectives: "Suppose you bought a tape recorder from a friend, it didn't work, and he refused to give your money back. How would you feel about this? Would it affect your friendship?" "Suppose you had promised to help a friend on some task, then had a chance to do something really fun and did that instead without telling your friend. How do you think the friend would feel? Would this affect the future of the friendship?" In short, it is hoped that the students will learn how their behavior influences other peoples' future responses.

Unit 20. Project Report on a Study to Improve a Friendship

Objective: Provide the students with another example of how a person can use the procedures to change their own and someone else's behavior.

Instructional Activities. This unit should be assigned as a package with Units 21 and 22. The students are asked to review the report and make a list of the mistakes they believe Julie made in conducting and writing up her project. You can use those ideas to begin the discussion of this unit and how the problems can be avoided when they conduct their own project in Unit 21.

Unit 21. A Behavior Analysis Project: Improving a Friendship

Objective: Conduct a behavior modification project designed to use positive procedures to improve a friendship.

BEHAVIOR MODIFICATION PROJECT: IMPROVING A FRIENDSHIP

Again, the important procedures here are positive reinforcement and extinction. The students are asked to analyze their interactions with a particular friend to see if there are behaviors that could be changed to improve it.

Instructional Activities. This is a relatively simple project, but there are three aspects of the procedure that need to be reviewed and rehearsed in class. First, this is an individualized project in which each student selects and defines the behaviors to be worked on. The students must write out behavioral definitions for the responses to be measured and changed. The instructor needs to review very carefully both how well defined and how appropriate these behaviors are. If the definitions are ambiguous or the selection of responses questionable, have the student rework them.

In Unit 19, the ideas of reciprocity and equity were discussed. These ideas have at their center the notion of fairness. The notion of fairness is a good issue to start the discussion of informed consent and ethics. There are two components of informed consent in the unit. First, the ethical issues of trying to change a friend's behavior need to be discussed. We all try to influence the behavior of friends, but in the study, the effort must be fair to the friend. The informed consent procedure is a way to ensure that this is the case. The actual interaction of asking for permission to conduct the project needs to be rehearsed. The way the project is explained will influence not only whether the other person will agree to participate but also the results of the project. The main points to make are that the project is designed to improve the friendship and that the student will be changing her/his own behavior also.

Finally, this is a long-running project, so the class will be covering other units while the students are conducting the project. As a consequence, the instructor will need to spend some time at the beginning of each class reviewing progress on these projects. You may also wish to schedule individual appointments with the students to review the projects. If a student is having difficulty, it is appropriate to change the procedure and have the student do something different.

Unit 22. Contracting and Negotiating

Objective: Teach the students how the idea of reciprocity can be used to negotiate agreements between groups of people.

CONTRACTING AND NEGOTIATING

Negotiation is the procedure used to develop a contract. A *contract* is an agreement between two people or groups; it specifies mutually acceptable responses and consequences for each. The effort in negotiation is to identify the desired consequences and behavior changes. In negotiation, all parties need to be calm and flexible. The resulting contract needs to be clear, specific, and objective.

NEWSPAPER ARTICLES

In contracting, it is important to be aware of, even if one does not necessarily agree with, the other person's perspective. The newspaper pieces are presented as a semihumorous view of the conflict between parents and adolescents. The pieces should be discussed not to convince the students that this view of them is correct but simply to show that there is another view.

Instructional Activities. After reviewing the study guide, you should briefly discuss the newspaper articles. The focus of concern here is understanding the other person's perspective (in this case the parents'). It is not necessary that you accept or agree with someone else's view of a situation, but it is important to recognize that he/she has one and that it may be different from yours.

Understanding the other person's position is important in negotiating a contract. A contract is based on the exchange of one set of goods or services for another. Money is often used as a medium of exchange, but it need not be. *Bartering* is a form of contracting that does not involve money; one service or commodity is directly exchanged for another. Because it is a simpler process, bartering can be used as an exercise to prepare the students to negotiate a behavioral contract. First, you need to divide the class into two groups and provide each group with a separate but equally desirable commodity. One easy method is to give one group several large bottles of soda pop and the other a couple of bags of snacks. The task then is for the students to negotiate a fair exchange of sodas for snacks. The hard part is arriving at a method of exchange that everyone feels is fair. From the exercise, the students should learn something about negotiating and the importance of being objective and arriving at a fair contract.

Finally, the students should role-play (practice) the process of negotiating a behavioral contract. A behavioral contract is essentially an exchange of services; I will do X, and you in turn will do Y. The students should go through all of the steps involved in the process. So the exercise will not be complete until there is a written contract. You can make up some hypothetical examples, or the students can suggest some problems; but avoid using ones that are too personal. The examples need not be restricted to adolescent–parent conflicts; contracting can be very useful between siblings or among friends. You should play the role of the adult in the first vignette and have one of the better students take the adolescent role. After the problem has been dealt with by negotiating a contract, discuss the process with the class, emphasizing the important points. Next, pair the students up and give them all the same problem to negotiate. When they have all finished a contract, compare the different contracts and discuss the strengths and weaknesses of each. The whole procedure can then be repeated with the second student in the pair now playing the role of the adolescent trying to negotiate a contract to solve a different problem.

The last and most important part of the unit is to have each student select a small problem to solve by negotiating a contract with their parents. The assignment will be to bring a signed contract to the next class session. You may wish to call the students' parents to explain the exercise and ask them to cooperate. Be sure to review the contracts at the beginning of the next meeting. Also, if there are any problems, help the students to correct them. Periodically, you will need to check with the students on how their contracts are working and to encourage them to keep trying.

Unit 23. Relaxation and Biofeedback

Objective: Discuss the notion of tension, and teach the students the technique called "progressive relaxation" that can be used to reduce the feeling of tension.

TENSION

Tension is a very poorly defined psychological concept, but in general, it refers to being inappropriately aroused. In the unit on emotions, ANS arousal was discussed in detail, with a particular focus on anxiety.

Tension appears to be a slightly different form of conditioned arousal. When we say we are tense, it usually means we can't relax. Rather, we are ready for vigorous activity. While anxiety is a form of conditioned fear, tension likely is a form of conditioned anger. As a consequence, when a person reports being tense, he/she is more likely to act out or behave aggressively.

RELAXATION

Autonomic nervous system (ANS) arousal is probably a type of continuum that runs from a high level (tense–aroused) to low (relaxed–nonaroused). We most often function between those extremes; for example, while I am writing this section, I am neither tense nor relaxed. So relaxation is a low level of arousal, below that at which we normally function. When a person is relaxed, he/she is less likely to respond strongly to most stimuli. That is, weak or even moderate stimuli that would produce a response if the person were tense will not do so if the person is relaxed. There are numerous physical analogies that you can use to illustrate this point in a concrete fashion; for example, the response produced by striking a drum head varies as a function of the surface tension, with considerable force being required to produce a tone if the head is slack. (Actually the notion of psychological tension is an analogy to the concept of tension in physics.) Therefore, if a person can learn to relax, he/she will be less likely to "lose" his/her temper and engage in inappropriate behavior.

Instructional Activities. The main task for the unit is to actually learn how to relax. The instructions presented in the students' workbook do, in fact, work. Anyone who systemically practices these steps will learn to be able to relax voluntarily. The key, of course, is practicing. So you will want to go through the exercise several times in class to get the students started. Also, encourage them to practice at home and ask them to self-monitor their progress.

Once the students are fairly good at quickly relaxing, you can set up some situations in which the students take turns being exposed to mildly aversive situations that would have provoked an aggressive response in the past. You must use your good judgment here. The objective here is to teach the students to use their new relaxation skills in situations in which they had difficulty in the past. By using mildly aversive stimuli such as negative comments, the student will have a chance to make the new responses; however, if the comments are too strong, the student may quickly become angry rather than relaxed.

After the students have been successful at relaxing in the fairly stressful situations, you can systematically increase the aversiveness of the negative comments. At each step, make sure that the student can still relax and is not becoming tense. In this fashion, it should be possible for the students to learn to relax in situations that in the past would have made them tense and angry.

A technique that should make this process more effective is to have the students construct individualized lists of things that make them tense. They should arrange their lists of situations in an increasing order of how tense each situation makes them. You can then use the lists to generate the situations to be practiced within the relaxation training.

Unit 24. Self-Management

Objective: Teach the students how to analyze and deal with self-management problems.

IMMEDIATE AND DELAYED CONSEQUENCES OF BEHAVIOR

For the most part, the analysis of self-management problems is based on the concepts and procedures discussed in previous units; the major new concept introduced in the unit has to do with the difference between immediate and delayed consequences for a response. A self-management problem occurs when there is a conflict between the immediate and delayed consequences of a response. For example, the immediate consequence of smoking is pleasurable; but the delayed consequence may be serious health problems. Similarly the immediate consequence of telling a lie may be avoiding punishment or an embarrassing situation, but the delayed consequences could be serious problems with parents or the loss of a friend. In these examples, the immediate consequences of the behavior (positive or negative reinforcement) increased the frequency of the response, but the delayed consequences are serious problems. The difficulty is that immediate consequences are more powerful in influencing behavior than delayed ones even though the delayed consequences may be more important.

As this unit and the examples of self-management projects that follow indicate, the first step in self-management is analyzing the problem in terms of the situation or discriminative stimuli and the immediate consequences for the problem behavior. Once this analysis has been completed, it is possible to decide how to change the behavior. The modification might involve changing or eliminating the discriminative stimulus, changing or eliminating the immediate consequence of the response, and/or trying to learn an alternative or incompatible response. The steps in a self-management project are (1) analyzing by collecting baseline data, (2) planning an intervention based on the analysis, (3) modifying the environment, and (4) finally evaluating the change in behavior to see if the program worked. An important substep in a project is that if the first plan doesn't work, the person must reanalyze the problem and modify the intervention procedures.

Instructional Activities. This unit and the next three are designed to give the students enough information so that they can design and conduct their own projects. At this point in the program, they should have all of the required skills. It is now a matter of showing them how to use those skills systematically to deal with their own behavior.

The instructor and the students should analyze the example in this unit and the sample student projects. The students then should try to produce other examples of self-control problems. Once an example is given, the class can analyze it in terms of the three factors discussed earlier (stimulus control, immediate versus delayed consequences, and alternative responses). After the analysis is completed, a plan for changing the behavior can be developed. Before moving on to Unit 28, in which the students are required to design their own projects, at least two and possibly more problems not discussed in the book should be analyzed and intervention plans designed. Problem responses such as not completing homework, having a messy room, fighting with teachers, and lying to friends are all difficulties that can be analyzed as self-management problems.

Unit 25. Fear of Public Speaking; Unit 26. Weight Control; Unit 27. Impatience; Unit 28. Decreasing Sarcastic Remarks

Objective: Demonstrate to the students how the manual's procedures and ideas can be used to change their own behavior.

Instructional Activities. No new concepts or procedures are introduced in these units. They are presented so that the students have examples of how a self-management project is done. One technique that should be emphasized in the discussion is the development of alternative behaviors. In earlier units, these were called "incompatible responses." When you are trying to change your own behavior, it is very difficult simply to stop doing something. It is much easier if there are specific alternative responses the person can now make in the situation. The good habits versus bad habits in Peggy's report and Kim's use of alternative activities instead of being impatient are examples of this idea.

Unit 29. Designing and Conducting a Self-Management Project

Objective: Assist the students to design, conduct, and evaluate a self-management project.

Instructional Activities. Again, this unit involves individual projects; the instructor's role is that of a consultant to the students. The students will work independently on these projects. Class time should be spent writing out plans and analyzing information. The instructor will be available to the students for advice and feedback. The *more* you can get the students *to write out their plans and record their data,* the easier it will be for you to evaluate whether they need assistance and what assistance to give.

Units 30–33. Smoking and Alcohol

These units cover two very important self-control, health, and social problems: smoking and drinking alcoholic beverages. In these units, we have attempted to present objective information to the student about these issues. It is recommended that the topics be treated in a "neutral" manner. We are not advocating a moral position on these behaviors, rather one that is scientifically defensible. There are no specific exercises other than those contained in the units. The approach taken to these units will depend on your local situation and the purpose of the course. We have used these materials with adolescents who have had difficulties with alcohol and other illegal substances, but that instruction took place within the context of a larger treatment program. As noted in the introduction, the basic educational approach described in this guide is not appropriate in and of itself for working with adolescents who have major problems. Further, for a variety of reasons, none of the research we have done to date in the area of substance abuse has been publishable. As a consequence, it is not possible to detail with any confidence the procedures for using these materials in such a project. Nonetheless, if you are interested in trying to design a program in the substance abuse area, simply write me, and I will provide as much information as I can.

For a regular self-management course, these units are meant to be mainly informational and possibly preventive in the broadest sense. Thus, no instructions are provided on how to do a self-management project on alcohol consumption. On the other hand, while it is not an easy task, a number of students have used self-management procedures to stop smoking, and an example is presented in Unit 29.

The suggested instructional activities presented in the guide, and the concepts and procedures discussed in the students' workbook are the products of considerable work. The program, however, is not a completed project. Every time I work with the workbook, talk to adolescents, try to teach someone else how to teach the course, I realize how much more research needs to be done. The collaborators required to improve the program are you, the instructors. I sincerely want to hear from you about how you are using the materials, what procedures seem to work, and especially what doesn't work. Good luck!!!

References

Ahlgren, A., Normen, A. A., Hochhauser, M., & Garvin, J. (1982). Antecedents of smoking among pre-adolescents. *Journal of Drug Education, 12*, 325–340.

Alexander, J. F. (1974). Behavior modification and delinquent youth. In R. E. Hardy & J. G. Gull (Eds.), *Psychological and vocational rehabilitation of the youthful offender*. Springfield, IL: Charles C. Thomas.

Alexander, J. F., & Parsons, B. U. (1973). Short term behavioral intervention with delinquent families. *Behavior Therapy, 1*, 4–32.

Bachman, J. G., Johnston, L. D., & O'Malley, P. M. (1981). Smoking, drinking, and drug use among American high school students: Correlates and trends, 1975–1979. *American Journal of Public Health, 71*, 59–69.

Bandura, A. (1969). *Principles of behavior modification*. New York: Holt, Rinehart & Winston.

Bandura, A. (1971). *Social learning theory*. Englewood Cliffs, NJ: Prentice-Hall.

Bandura, A. (1975). Self-reinforcement: Theoretical and methodological considerations. *Behaviorism, 4*, 135–155.

Bandura, A. (1977). Self-efficacy: Toward a unifying theory of behavioral change. *Psychological Review, 84*(2), 191–215.

Bandura, A., & Mahoney, M. J. (1974). Maintenance and transfer of self-reinforcement functions. *Behaviour Research and Therapy, 12*, 89–97.

Barker, R. G. (1968). *Ecological psychology*. Stanford, CA: Stanford University Press.

Barlow, D., Hayes, S., & Nelson, R. (1984). *The scientist practitioner: Research and accountability in clinical and educational settings*. New York: Pergamon.

Barrish, H., Saunders, M., & Wolf, M. (1969). Good Behavior Game: Effects of individual contingencies for group consequences on disruptive behavior in a classroom. *Journal of Applied Behavior Analysis, 2*, 119–124.

Becker, W. (1986). *Applied psychology for teachers: A behavioral cognitive approach*. Chicago: Science Research Associates.

Becker, W., & Engelmann, S. (1978). Systems for basic instruction: Theory and applications. In A. C. Catania & T. A. Brigham (Eds.), *Handbook of applied behavior analysis*. New York: Irvington.

Biglan, A., Hops, H., Faller, C., Ary, D., Friedman, L., Nautel, C., & Weissman, W. (1983, August). *Methodological considerations in studying the smoking acquisition process*. Paper presented at the meeting of the American Psychological Association, Anaheim, CA.

Bland, J. M., Bewly, B. R., & Day, I. (1980). Primary school boys: Image of self and smoker. *British Journal of Preventive Social Medicine, 9*, 27–30.

Braukmann, C. J., Fixsen, D. L., Phillips, E. L., & Wolf, M. M. (1975). Behavioral approaches to treatment in the crime and delinquency field. *Criminology, 13*, 299–331.

Brigham, T. A. (1978). Self-control. In A. C. Catania & T. A. Brigham (Eds.), *Handbook of applied behavior analysis.* New York: Irvington.

Brigham, T. A. (1979). Some effects of choice on academic performance. In L. Perlmuter & R. Monty (Eds.), *Choice and locus of control.* Englewood Cliffs, NJ: Erlbaum.

Brigham, T. A., Contreras, J. A., Handel, G. S., & Castillo, A. O. (1983). A comparison of two approaches for improving social and job placement skills. *Behavioral Engineering, 8*, 104–115.

Brigham, T. A., Hopper, C., Hill, B., de Armas, A., & Newsom, P. (1985). A self-management program for disruptive adolescents in the school: A clinical replication analysis. *Behavior Therapy, 16*, 99–115.

Canter, A., & Canter, C. (1976). *Assertive discipline.* Los Angeles: Canter and Associates.

Catania, A. C. (1976) The myth of self-reinforcement. In T. A. Brigham, R. Hawkins, J. Scott, & T. F. McLaughlin (Eds.), *Behavior analysis in education: Self-control and reading.* Dubuque, IA: Kendall/Hunt.

Danaher, B., & Lichtenstein, E. (1978). *Become an ex-smoker.* Englewood Cliffs, NJ: Prentice-Hall.

de Armas, A., & Kelly, J. (1987). Social relationships in adolescence: Issues in skills development and strategies for intervention. In J. Worell & F. Danner (Eds.), *Adolescent development: Issues for education.* New York: Academic Press.

de Armas, A., Kern, T. G., & Brigham, T. A. (1986, May). *Self-management and social skills training with adjudicated delinquents.* Paper presented at the meeting of the Association for Behavior Analysis, Milwaukee.

Dethier, V. G. (1962). *To know a fly.* San Francisco: Holden-Day.

Dillashaw, F. G., & Okey, J. R. (1980). Test of integrated science process skills for secondary science students. *Science Education, 65*(5), 601–608.

Douds, A. F., Engelsterd, M., & Collingwood, T. R. (1977). Behavior contracting with youthful offenders and their parents. *Child Welfare, 56*, 409–417.

Evans, R. I. (1976). Smoking in children: Developing a social–psychological strategy of deterrence. *Journal of Preventive Medicine, 5*, 122–127.

Evans, R. I., Rozelle, R. M., Mittelmark, M. B., Hansen, W. B., Bane, A. L., & Havis, J. (1978). Deterring the onset of smoking in children: Knowledge of immediate psychological effects and coping with peer pressure, media pressure, and parent modeling. *Journal of Applied Social Psychology, 8*, 126–136.

Feldman, P. (1983). Juvenile offending: Behavioral approaches to prevention and intervention. *Child and Family Behavior Therapy, 5*(1), 37–50.

Ferber, H., Keeley, S. M., & Shemberg, K. M. (1974). Training parents in behavior modification: Outcome of and problems encountered in a program after Patterson's work. *Behavior Therapy, 5*, 415–419.

Fixsen, D., Phillips, E., & Wolf, M. M. (1978). Mission-orientation behavior research: The teaching family model. In A. C. Catania & T. A. Brigham (Eds.), *Handbook of applied behavior analysis.* New York: Irvington.

Freedman, B. J., Rosenthal, L., Donahoe, C. P., Jr., Schlundt, D. G., & McFall, R. M. A. (1978). A social behavior analysis of skill deficits in delinquent and nondelinquent adolescent boys. *Journal of Consulting and Clinical Psychology, 46*, 1448–1462.

Freud, S. (1930/1962). *Civilization and its discontents.* New York: W. W. Norton.

Goldstein, A. P., & Kanfer, F. H. (1979). *Maximizing treatment gains.* New York: Academic Press.

Gordon, T. (1981). Crippling our children with discipline. *Journal of Education, 4,* 228–243.

Goyette, C. H., Connors, C. K. & Ulrich, R. F. (1978). Normative data on Revised Connors Parent and Teacher Rating Scores. *Journal of Abnormal Child Psychology, 6,* 221–236.

Graubard, P., Rosenberg, H., & Miller, M. (1974). Ecological approaches to social deviancy. In R. Ulrich, T. Stachnick, & J. Mabry (Eds.), *Control of human behavior* (Vol. 3). Glenview, IL: Scott Foresman.

Greenspoon, J. (1955). The reinforcing effect of two spoken sounds on the frequency of two responses. *American Journal of Psychology, 68,* 409–416.

Gross, A. (1982). Self-management training and medication compliance in children with diabetes. *Child and Family Behavior Therapy, 4,* 47–55.

Gross, A., & Brigham, T. A. (1980). Self-delivered consequences versus desensitization in the treatment of fear of rats. *Journal of Clinical Psychology, 43,* 384–390.

Gross, A., Brigham, T. A., Hopper, C., & Bologna, N. (1980). Self-management and social skills training: A study with predelinquent and delinquent youth, *Criminal Justice and Behavior, 7,* 161–184.

Gross, A., Magalnick, L., & Richardson, P. (1985). Self-management training with families of insulin-dependent diabetic children: A controlled long-term investigation. *Child and Family Behavior Therapy, 7,* 35–50.

Gross, A., & Wojnilower, D. (1985). Self-directed behavior change in children: Is it self-directed? *Behavior Therapy, 15,* 501–514.

Hansen, W. B., & Evans, R. I. (1982). Feedback versus information concerning carbon monoxide as an early intervention strategy in adolescent smoking. *Adolescence, 17,* 89–98.

Harney, M. K., Brigham, T. A., & Sanders, M. (1986). Design and systematic evaluation of the freshman athlete scholastic training program. *Journal of Counseling Psychology, 33,* 454–461.

Hartig, M., & Kanfer, F. H. (1973). The role of verbal self-instructions in children's resistance to temptation. *Journal of Personality and Social Psychology, 25,* 259–267.

Hoefler, S. A., & Bornstein, P. H. (1975). Achievement Place: An evaluative review. *Criminal Justice and Behavior, 2,* 146–148.

Hopkins, R., Mauss, A., Kearney, K., & Weisheit, R. (1987). Comprehensive evaluation of a model alcohol education curriculum. *Journal of Studies on Alcohol, 48,* 419–431.

Jaynes, J. (1977). *The origins of consciousness in the breakdown of the bicameral mind.* Boston: Houghton Mifflin.

Johnston, L. D., Bachman, J. G., & O'Malley, P. M. (1977). Drug use among American high school students, 1975–1977. Rockville, MD: National Institute on Drug Abuse.

Jones, R. R., Weinrott, M. R., & Howard, J. R. (1981). *The national evaluation of the Teaching Family model.* Final report to NIMH Center for Studies in Crime and Delinquency.

Kanfer, F., Karoly, P., & Newman, A. (1975). Reduction of children's fear of the dark by competence-related and situational threat-related verbal cues. *Journal of Consulting and Clinical Psychology, 43,* 251–258.

Kanfer, F., & Phillips, J. S. (1970). *Learning foundations of behavior therapy.* New York: Wiley.

Karoly, P., & Briggs, N. Z. (1978). Effects of rules and directed delays on components of children's inhibitionary self-control. *Journal of Experimental Child Psychology*, *26*, 267–279.

Karoly, P., & Steffen, J. J. (Eds.). (1980). *Improving the long term effects of psychotherapy*. New York: Gardner Press.

Kern, T. G., & de Armas, A. (1986, May). *Behavioral self-management training with disabled learning students*. Paper presented at the meeting of the Association for Advancement of Behavior Therapy, Chicago.

Kifer, R. E., Lewis, M. A., Green, D. R., & Phillips, E. L. (1974). Training predelinquent youths and their parents to negotiate conflict situations. *Journal of Applied Behavior Analysis*, *7*, 357–364.

Kirigin, K. A., Braukmann, C., Atwater, J., & Wolf, M. M. (1982). An evaluation of teaching family (Achievement Place) group honors for juvenile offenders. *Journal of Applied Behavior Analysis*, *15*, 1–16.

Kirigin, K. A., Phillips, E. L., Timbers, G. D., Fixsen, D. L., & Wolf, M. M. (1977). Achievement Place: The modification of academic behavior problems of youths in a group home setting. In B. Etzel, J. M. LeBlanc, & D. M. Baer (Eds.), *New developments in behavioral research: Theory, method, and application*. Hillsdale, NJ: Erlbaum.

Lerman, P. (1968). Evaluative studies of institutions for delinquents: Implications for research and social policy. *Social Work*, *13*, 55–64.

Leventhal, H., & Cleary, P. D. (1980). The smoking problem: A review of the research and theory in behavioral risk modification. *Psychological Bulletin*, *88*, 370–405.

Lewin, K. (1953). The field theory approach to adolescence. In J. M. Seidman (Ed.), *The adolescent: A book of readings*. New York: Holt, Rinehart & Winston.

Liberman, R. P., Ferris, C., Salgado, P., & Salgado, J. (1975). Replication of the Achievement Place model in California. *Journal of Applied Behavior Analysis*, *8*, 282–299.

Lovaas, O. I. (1973). *Behavioral treatment of autistic children*. Morristown, NJ: General Learning Press.

Mahoney, M. J. (1974). *Cognition and behavior modification*. Cambridge, MA: Ballinger.

Maloney D. M., Harper, T. M., Braukmann, C. J., Fixsen, D. L., Phillips, E. L. & Wolf, M. M. (1976). Teaching conversation-related skills to predelinquent girls. *Journal of Applied Behavior Analysis*, *9*, 371.

Mauss, A., Hopkins, R., Weisheit, R., & Kearney, K. (1987). The problematic prospects for prevention in the classroom: Should alcohol education programs be expected to reduce drinking by youth? *Journal of Studies on Alcohol*, *48*, 472–490.

McAlister, A., Perry, C., Killen, J., Slinkard, L. A., & Maccoby, N. (1980). Pilot study of smoking, alcohol, and drug abuse prevention. *American Journal of Public Health*, *70*, 719–721.

McKennell, A., & Bynner, J. (1969). Self-images and smoking behavior among school boys. *British Journal of Educational Psychology*, *39*, 27–39.

Meichenbaum, D. (1977). *Cognitive-behavior modification*. New York: Plenum.

Meier, S. E., Brigham, T. A., & Handel, G. (1984). Effects of feedback on legally intoxicated drivers. *Journal of Studies on Alcohol*, *45*(6), 528–533.

Miller, L. K. (1981). *Principles of everyday behavior analysis*. Monterey, CA: Brooks/Cole.

National Institutes of Health. (1976). *Teenage smoking, national pattern of cigarette smoking, ages 12 through 18, in 1972 and 1974*. U.S. Department of Health, Education and Welfare; Public Health Service; DHEW Publication No. (NIH) 76-931, 125.

Newman, J. (1971). Ninth grade smokers—two years later. University of Illinois anti-smoking educational study. *Journal of School Health, 41,* 497–501.

Niemann, J., & Brigham, T. A. (1976, May). *The development and experimental validation of a course in self-management for sixth graders.* Paper presented at the meeting of the Association for Behavior Analysis, Milwaukee.

O'Leary, S., & Dubey, D. R. (1979). Applications of self-control procedures by children: A review. *Journal of Applied Behavior Analysis, 12,* 449–466.

Patterson, G. R. (1974). Interventions for boys with conduct problems: Multiple settings, treatments, and criteria. *Journal of Consulting and Clinical Psychology, 42,* 471–482.

Patterson, G. R., & Gullion, M. E. (1971). *Living with children.* Champaign, IL: Research Press.

Patterson, G. R., & Reid, J. B. (1973). Interventions for families of aggressive boys: A replication study. *Behaviour Research and Therapy, 11,* 383–394.

Perry, C. L., Killen, J. D., Slinkard, L. A., & McAlister, A. L. (1980). Peer teaching and smoking prevention among junior high school students. *Adolescence, 15,* 277–281.

Phillips, E. L. (1968). Achievement Place: Token economy reinforcement procedures in a home style rehabilitation setting for predelinquent boys. *Journal of Applied Behavior Analysis, 1,* 213–222.

President's Commission on Law Enforcement and Administration of Justice. (1967). *Task force reports: Corrections.* Washington, DC: U.S. Printing Office.

President's Commission on Law Enforcement and Administration of Justice. (1967). *Task force reports: Juvenile delinquency of youth crime.* Washington, DC: U.S. Government Printing Office.

Rachlin, H. (1970). *Introduction to modern behaviorism.* San Francisco: Freeman.

Rachlin, H. (1977). Reinforcing and punishing thoughts. *Behavior Therapy, 8,* 659–665.

Rachlin, H., & Green, L. (1972). Commitment, choice, and self-control procedures by children: A review. *Journal of Applied Behavior Analysis, 17,* 15–22.

Rapaport, A. (1953). *Operational Philosophy.* New York: Wiley.

Rehm, L. P., & Marston, A. R. (1968). Reduction of social anxiety through modification of self-reinforcement. *Journal of Consulting and Clinical Psychology, 32,* 565–574.

Reppucci, N., & Saunders, J. (1974). Social psychology of behavior modification: Problems of implementation in natural settings. *American Psychologist, 29,* 649–660.

Roff, M. (1961). Childhood social relations and young adult bad conduct. *Journal of Abnormal and Social Psychology, 65,* 333–337.

Roff, M., Sells, S. B., & Golden, M. (1972). *Social adjustment and personality development in children.* Minneapolis: University of Minnesota Press.

Rotter, J. B. (1972). Generalized expectancies for internal versus external control of reinforcement. In J. B. Rotter, J. E. Chance, & J. Phares (Eds.), *Applications of a social learning theory of personality.* New York: Holt, Rinehart & Winston.

Salzinger, K., Feldman, R. S., & Portnoy, S. (1970). Training parents of brain-injured children in the use of operant conditioning procedures. *Behavior Therapy, 1,* 4–32.

Sherif, M., & Sherif, C. W. (1964). *Exploration into conformity and deviation of adolescents: Reference groups.* New York: Harper & Row.

Sidman, M. (1960). *Tactics of scientific research.* New York: Basic Books.

Skinner, B. F. (1948). *Walden two.* New York: Macmillan.

Skinner, B. F. (1953). *Science and human behavior.* New York: Macmillan.

Skinner, B. F. (1956). A case history in scientific method. *American Psychologist, 11,* 221–233.

Skinner, B. F. (1966). An operant analysis of problem solving. In B. Kleinmuntz (Ed.), *Problem solving: Research, method, and theory.* New York: Wiley.

Skinner, B. F. (1971). *Beyond freedom and dignity.* New York: Knopf.

Skinner, B. F. (1974). *About behaviorism.* New York: Knopf.

Snyder, J., & White, M. (1979). The use of cognitive self-instruction in the treatment of behaviorally disturbed adolescents. *Behavior Therapy, 10,* 227–235.

Spence, S. (1982). Social skills training with adolescent offenders. In M. P. Feldman (Ed.), *Developments in the study of criminal behavior* (Vol. 1). Chichester, England: Wiley.

Stokes, T., & Baer, D. M. (1977). An implicit technology of generalization. *Journal of Applied Analysis, 10,* 349–358.

Stuart, R. B. (1971). Behavioral contracting within the families of delinquents. *Journal of Behavior Therapy and Experimental Psychiatry, 2,* 1–11.

Stuart, R. B., Jayaratyne, S., & Tripodi, T. (1976). Changing adolescent deviant behavior through reprogramming the behavior of parents and teachers: An experimental evaluation. *Canadian Journal of Behavioural Science, 8,* 133–144.

Stuart, R. B., & Lott, L. A. (1972). Behavioral contracting with delinquents. A cautionary note. *Journal of Behavior Therapy and Experimental Psychiatry, 3,* 161–169.

Timbers, G. D., Timbers, V. D., Fixsen, D. L., Phillips, E. L., & Wolf, M. M. (1973, August). *Token reinforcement, social reinforcement and instructional procedures in a family style treatment setting for predelinquent girls.* Paper presented at the meeting of the American Psychological Association, Montreal.

Tobin, K., & Capie, W. (1982). Relationship between formal reasoning ability, laws of control, academic engagement and integrated process skill achievement. *Journal of Research in Science Teaching, 19,* 113–121.

Watson, D. L., Tharp, R. G. (1972). *Self-directed behavior: Self-modification for personal adjustment.* Monterey, CA: Brooks/Cole.

Weathers, L., & Liberman, R. P. (1975). Contingency contracting with families of delinquent adolescents. *Behavior Therapy, 6,* 356–366.

Werner, J. S., Minikin, N., Minikin, B. L., Fixsen, D. L., Phillips, E. L., & Wolf, M. M. (1975). Intervention package: Analysis to prepare juvenile delinquents for encounters with police officers. *Criminal Justice and Behavior, 2,* 55–83.

Wiltz, N. A., & Patterson, G. R. (1974). An evaluation of parent training procedures designed to alter inappropriate aggressive behavior of boys. *Behavior Therapy, 5,* 215–221.

Wolf, M. M. (1978). Social validity: The case for subjective measurement or how applied behavior analysis is finding its heart. *Journal of Applied Behavior Analysis, 11,* 203–214.

Wolfgang, M. E., Figlio, R. M., & Sellin, T. (1972). *Delinquency in a birth cohort.* Chicago: University of Chicago Press.

Wood, B., & Brigham, T. A. (1987). Psychology as a first course in science for 8th graders. *Psychology in the Schools, 24,* 1–10.

Index